THE MEMORY ADVANTAGE

THE MEMORY ADVANTAGE

Improve the Way You Learn, Remember, Think and Feel

THOMAS H. CROOK, Ph.D.

SelectBooks, Inc.
New York

The Memory Advantage: Improving the Way You Learn, Remember, Think and Feel

©2006 SelectBooks, Inc.

This edition published by SelectBooks, Inc.
For information address SelectBooks, Inc., One Union Square West, New York, New York 10003

First Edition

ISBN-13: 978-59079-109-7
ISBN-10: 1-59079-109-6

Library of Congress Cataloging-in-Publication Data

Crook, Thomas.

The memory advantage : improve the way you learn, remember, think, and feel / Thomas H. Crook. — 1st ed.

p. cm.

ISBN-13: 978-1-59079-109-7 (alk. paper)

ISBN-10: 1-59079-109-6 (alk. paper)

1. Memory--Popular works. 2. Memory disorders—Prevention—Popular works.

I. Title.

QP406.C76 2006

612.8'23312—dc22

2006026251

Manufactured in the United States of America

10 9 8 7 6 5 4 3 2 1

This book is dedicated to my wife, Kay Grant–Crook.
I knew when I met her that she would be unforgettable.

Contents

Introduction

We have all had the experience of misplacing keys or reading glasses, forgetting someone's name just after we are introduced, or walking into a room and forgetting why we went there. Most middle-aged and older adults also realize that some abilities improve with age, but memory, like gymnastic or track and field skills, is not generally one of them. There are techniques for dealing with memory problems and they are part of what you will gain from *The Memory Advantage*. That is where virtually all memory books end, however, and we will go much further. We will consider how important memory is in how you think and feel about yourself and others, and, indeed, in who you are. We will see how memories can become your best friends and supporters or, when distorted, your worst enemies and detractors. You will learn how to use your memory to make yourself a clearer thinking, more self-confident, and happier person, and that will be your "Memory Advantage."

1

Understanding Memory

I began thinking about the concept of a memory advantage more than fifty years ago at St. Mary's School in Baltimore. My blessed but much feared third grade teacher, Sister Martha, had been teaching multiplication tables for quite a few weeks and was conducting speed drills by calling out multiplication problems. As she called out each problem she walked up and down every row in the classroom, ruler in hand, listening for tardy or incorrect responses. I had made a gentlemanly effort to learn the tables and was quite confident in my abilities to remember them ... as long as one of the two numbers being multiplied was four or lower. I had every intention of moving into the higher columns in due course, but had not yet found the time in my schedule. After only a few problems into the exercise, the chilling sound known to every Catholic School child of the day crackled through the room: that of ruler meeting knuckle. Suddenly, I regretted my hours watching Western movies or playing baseball after school. I vowed that, if only I could escape this exercise, I would go straight home and devote my life to arithmetic memorization. First, though, I had to conceal my less than perfect mastery of the multiplication tables. Simply moving my facial muscles was adequate so long as Sister Martha was on the other side of the room, but as she approached and focused her intense green eyes directly on me I could only hope that through divine intervention, at least one of the two numbers in the problem she was about to pose to me was four or lower. My palms began to sweat and I could feel my face turning red as I watched the numbers form on Sister Martha's lips. "Four times four" she shouted. As I confidently shouted back "sixteen," I felt the greatest sense of relief and elation imaginable. Either divine intervention or just good luck had saved me from an embarrassing and painful memory failure, and I vowed that after that afternoon's baseball game and 5:00 television Western I would learn the multiplication tables perfectly, and gain a memory advantage for Sister Martha's next sadistic arithmetic exercise.

There are many Sister Martha characters in the memory of all of us educated before today's kinder, gentler age of education. Back when rote memorization was the primary means of teaching almost everything, teachers were generally unconcerned about self-esteem and providing everyone with a good grade. Failure to memorize the facts you were taught led to punishment of one sort or another, usually including social ostracization. Of course what we recall must have been enlightened compared to earlier years because I do not recall a "dunce cap and chair," and the principal's paddle, while still a visible reminder of authority, was rarely employed, at least in the schools I attended. Even in schools today there is little alternative to rote memorization of a great deal of material and the consequences of poor learning and memory abilities become apparent early in childhood.

In some children, a memory advantage is provided genetically. Many years after Sister Martha, when I was a much more diligent student who actually studied the information to be recalled on a test, I spent hour after hour at my desk studying, which meant principally trying to memorize information. It seemed to me that it took me three or four hours, and often more, to memorize what a few of my friends could memorize in the classroom, without any homework at all. It was clear that my memory advantage was not going to come from genes. What followed was many years of simply spending hour after hour learning and memorizing written material.

So, a memory advantage can come from genes or from hard work, but it can also come from understanding more about the psychology and neurophysiology of memory; changes in memory that occur across the life span; medical, psychological, and lifestyle issues that affect memory; techniques and dietary supplements for improving memory; and how memory is much more important than you think. Memory controls what you think about yourself and others and, subsequently, your full range of emotions.

Let us begin by considering different types of memory and the anatomy and chemistry of memory.

Categories of Memory

Short-term Memory

During our waking hours we are constantly scanning visually, and through our other senses of hearing, touch, smell and taste. We scan millions of bits of information per minute and a very small part of that information enters short-term memory. The capacity of short term memory is very small, only about seven bits of information. For example, if I were to read to you a series of digits and ask you to repeat them back to me from memory, you would have no problem until the series length reached about five digits, and then you would have to concentrate. You might then be able to repeat back a list of seven, but probably would have difficulty going much beyond that. I could train you to increase the size of each bit by linking together numbers but the capacity of short-term memory would still remain quite small and the time information can be held is very brief. For information to be remembered more than a few seconds, it must be transferred into long-term memory.

Working Memory

There is an intermediary memory system where we can hold information just long enough to complete a task, without transferring it into long-term memory. We refer to this as *Working Memory*. We must keep information in working memory in our consciousness, and we must continue rehearsing it. For example, if someone gives my wife directions to a gas station that include various right and left turns at various landmarks (I would not need such directions), she may be able to remember them just long enough to find the station, as long as she keeps repeating them to herself. As soon as she found the station, that information will be discarded, gone forever. Working memory would also be involved in remembering a phone number just long enough to dial it.

Long-term Memory

There are at least two different types of long-term memory: *Declarative Memory*, or memory for facts or past experiences in life, and *Procedural Memory*, which is memory for skills. The vast majority of what we think of as information in long-term memory is in declarative memory and here we generally make a distinction between semantic memory and episodic memory.

Episodic memories are tied to particular events, times and places. Episodic memories might include your recollection of meeting your husband or wife, bringing your newborn babies home from the hospital, or speeding along the highway with the car's top down on a warm spring day. By contrast, semantic memory is context free and represents your general knowledge about the world. Information stored in semantic memory may combine multiple episodic memories and other information that forms a clear definition of an object or concept. For example, your concept of "child" may be influenced by many personal experiences as a child, as the parent of a child and so on, but these memories are combined and together with other information form the general concept of "child" in semantic memory.

Procedural memory involves memory for riding a bicycle, swimming, playing chess or crocheting. Procedural memory is highly resistant to forgetting, as old maxims such as "never forgetting how to ride a bike" suggest. Dr. Daniel Schacter, a renowned psychologist at Harvard University, once took a patient with advanced Alzheimer's disease out on the golf course. Frederick was a life-long golfer and remembered all the proper procedures for teeing up the ball, choosing the appropriate club, swinging smoothly, marking his ball, and so on. He also had an excellent golf vocabulary, correctly using words such as "birdie" and "dogleg." However, at the end of each round, Frederick had no recollection of having played any holes, and when asked a week later to play again he responded by saying that he was a little nervous because he hadn't played in months.

Remote Memory

Remote Memory is the repository for "unforgettable" experiences. These may be many decades old, going back to early childhood, such as my memory of the third grade and Sister Martha. My mother-in-law, Thelma Grant, who is eighty-eight years old, once demonstrated how effective remote memory can be even while much more recently learned information may be forgotten. She rummaged through a box of photographs that she hadn't seen in many years and found her junior high school graduation photograph. She then proceeded to name each of the fifty or so graduates and tell a detailed story about each. She then turned to my wife and said, "Well that was fun but I guess you and ...[long pause]... what's-his-name will have to be leaving pretty soon."

Areas of the Brain Involved in Memory

The largest part of the brain is the cerebrum and it is divided into two halves, or hemispheres. The right hemisphere controls the left side of the body and the left hemisphere controls the right side. The hemispheres are connected at the *corpus callosum,* a band of some 300 million nerve fibers. There is some distinction between the hemispheres in right-handed people in that the left hemisphere is more closely associated with verbal/logical thought while the right hemisphere is associated more closely with visual and spatial tasks.

A one-eighth-inch thick, intricately folded layer of nerve cells covers the cerebrum and this is the cortex (Latin for *bark*). The cortex allows us to remember, to analyze and compare incoming information with stored information, to organize experiences, to learn languages, to make decisions and perform myriad other cognitive tasks.

It is not at all unusual for an individual to be talented when performing tasks controlled by one hemisphere of the cortex and normal, or even deficient in performing tasks controlled by the other. In that case, one is said to be *right* or *left hemisphere dominant.* I, for example, struggle with many mechanical and visual-spatial tasks and found engineering courses in high school and college very difficult, while English, history, economics, philosophy and psychology were quite interesting and easy to learn. Thus, I was left-hemisphere dominant, but that is certainly not the case in everyone. Many males and some females are right-hemisphere dominant and make talented mechanics and engineers, although they might struggle in writing a letter and never touch a crossword puzzle.

Knowing if one shows hemispheric dominance may be useful early in life. I once tested a young lady who was struggling in the eleventh grade of a Catholic school that would have been as alien as Mars to Sister Martha. This school, Archbishop Spaulding High School in Severn, Maryland, had given the young lady, Carol, every advantage possible. They gave her more time on tests than others, and when her test scores did not improve, they let her take open-book tests when everyone else was tested from memory. Finally, they let Carol take the tests home, along with her books and work on them there. Still, she struggled.

I saw Carol and her distraught mother and administered a number of tests, including a widely used intelligence test that has both verbal and "performance" subscales. The performance scales require that you manipulate objects, solve puzzles and so on. They are not dependent on verbal learning and memory. Consistent with her academic record, Carol scored far below normal on the verbal tasks and showed evidence of a profound verbal learning and memory disorder. However, she performed exceptionally well on the performance tests measuring visual spatial abilities. One test, for example, requires that red blocks painted diagonally white on some sides be arranged so as to form an overall design shown by the examiner drawn on a card. The designs get increasingly difficult and intricate as the test proceeds and most people fail well before the most difficult design is reached.

Carol completed all the exercises within the allotted time. This was one of eleven subscales in the most widely used intelligence scale of the time (it has been revised slightly since), so her performance was consistent on that scale with the highest IQ obtainable, even though she had performed on several verbal subscales at a level associated with a profound learning impairment. Her mother reported that Carol was the family "engineer," and was not only able to install all new electronic devices while barely consulting instructions, but could figure out any problem that arose on the family computer. Armed with this new knowledge, Carol's parents could plot her academic future. She would continue to struggle in high school, although we could restructure the way she attempted to memorize by using more visual than verbal techniques. She graduated (just barely) with her class. But then the world changed for Carol. She went off to a private two year school of design and specialized in computer graphics. She became the bright student helping others, a complete role reversal. Now, sixteen years later, Carol is a successful graphic designer living with her husband and children in New Hampshire.

The cortex of each hemisphere is divided into four areas referred to as lobes.

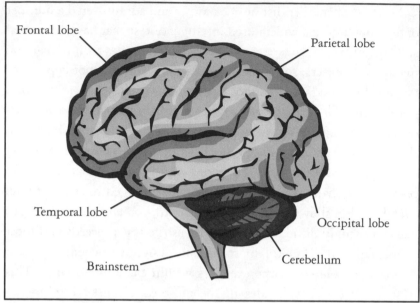

Figure 1. The four lobes of the brain

The lobes are specialized according to the type of information they store and process. For example, the largest of the four lobes, the frontal lobes, are associated with the performance of higher level cognitive functions including organization, planning, decision making and problem solving. Critical information related to these tasks is stored in the frontal lobes. The parietal lobes extend from the ear to the top of the head. They receive information from touch and are involved in the formation of some memories. The occipital lobes, located at the back of the head, are sometimes referred to as the visual cortex, and are responsible for visually mediated memory. The temporal lobes fit under the temporal bone above the ears and are involved with hearing, perception and, of particular importance, semantic memory.

Beneath the cortex is a group of cellular structures known as the limbic system. These structures, particularly the hypothalamus, control many basic body functions and also emotional responses. Several of these structures are of critical importance in memory.

First is an area of the limbic system referred to as the hippocampus (pronounced as you would guess, hippo campus). Actually, there are two hippocampi, one in each hemisphere. This area has been very extensively investigated during the past several decades and is a structure shaped like a seahorse buried deep in the temporal lobes. (The word itself is Greek for seahorse.) These are critical structures in forming *some* new memories. For example, the hippocampus is very important in forming *new* episodic memories, but appears to play no role at all in procedural memories. The hippocampus is also involved in spatial or navigational memory.

Another limbic structure, also in the temporal lobes, just in front of the hippocampus, is an almond shaped structure labeled the amygdala (pronounced am ig du la). Like the hippocampus, the amygdala (Greek for almond) helps transfer information from short-term to long-term memory. Its main function seems to be that of linking memories that were formed through several senses. The amygdala also plays an important role in the formation and storage of memories with high emotional value. It is the amygdala that is responsible for indelible memories of events that may have occurred recently or many decades ago. The vivid image that is almost certainly in the minds of almost all Americans of where they were and what they were doing on the morning of September 11, 2001 is testimony to the power of the amygdala in what we remember.

A tragic case illustrates how delicate the interplay is among these memory structures. This is the well known case of HM, a twenty-seven-year-old man in 1953 suffering from intractable epileptic seizures. A Connecticut neurosurgeon, Dr William Scoville, in an attempt to halt or at least diminish the seizures, removed structures from the temporal lobes on both sides of HM's brain. He removed the hippocampus, the amygdala, and parts of some neighboring areas of temporal cortex. He had performed the first known bi-lateral, medial, temporal lobectomy. Immediately after the surgery, it was clear that it had produced profound memory problems. Although the seizures were reduced somewhat and HM could speak and converse normally, he had no idea where he was, to whom he was speaking, or what he had been doing five minutes earlier. HM's memory for events preceding the surgery remained largely intact, but his episodic and much of his semantic memory for events following the surgery was destroyed. He is still alive, but he can recall no one he has met and no experience he has had for more than a half century. HM lives truly alone.

Memory under the Microscope

So, we have seen areas of the brain that are particularly important for memory, but let us see how memories are formed at a microscopic level. First, the basic unit of the brain is the nerve cell, or neuron. There are about 100 billion neurons in the brain and about twice that number of cells to provide structure and metabolic support to the neurons. These latter cells are referred to as *neuroglia,* or simply *glia.* Neurons are surrounded by a cell membrane and have

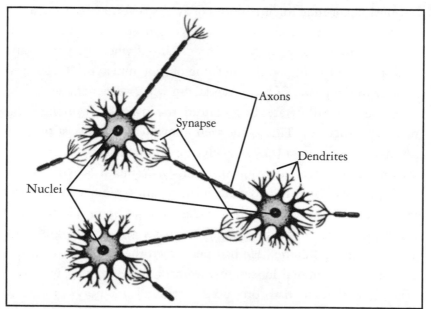

Figure 2. Neurons

a very thin filament, an axon. Projecting from the end of the axon and from the edge of the cell body are many other small filaments known as dendrites. Dendrites on the cell body are like antennae that receive electrical impulses from other cells and conduct them along to the cell's center. Dendrites on the axon conduct nerve impulses to other neurons. Each axon and dendrite has many contact points so that it may communicate with thousands of other neurons. Each specialized contact point is a very small space referred to as a synapse and a single neuron can have 100,000 synapses connecting it to other neurons. Messages from one neuron to another travel down the axon in the form of electrical impulses which release chemicals, referred to as neurotransmitters, when they reach the synapse. These chemicals travel across the ultra-microscopic space, reach the dendrites of the next neuron, and activate specific receptors in a "lock and key" fashion. There are many different neurotransmitters, and some such as *acetylcholine*, which we will discuss later, are particularly important in memory formation. This transmission is repeated almost instantaneously across hundreds or thousands of neurons, and memories are stored not in the neurons or synapses themselves, but in the *pattern* of connections between neurons that is modified by each transmission. Thus, long-term memory storage involves the growth of new synaptic connections between neurons throughout the cortex and other critical areas of the brain.

This last paragraph sounds fairly straightforward, but only a decade or so ago scientific doctrine held that neurons cannot regenerate and that synaptic sprouting, or arborization, was not possible. The idea that memories do not reside in fixed places, but are created as new patterns of synaptic connections are formed among neurons, would have been scoffed at years ago when I was a young graduate student. Today, we can see the actual neuronal changes and new interconnections among neurons that occur when new memories are formed.

An interesting example of how neuronal growth occurs in areas of the brain related to particular types of memory as those areas are extensively used is provided by a recent study of London taxi drivers. Unlike the United States, drivers of London's classic black taxis are extraordinarily well trained. They must know literally every road and major establishment in the city. Training generally lasts three or four years and three quarters of prospective drivers are unable to complete the course. You will recall that the hippocampus is involved in navigational skills (in both birds and mammals), particularly the posterior portion of the hippocampus. When a group of London taxi drivers and a group of comparable non-drivers were given Magnetic Resonance Image (MRI) scans of the brain, the former group had significantly larger posterior hypocampi. Beyond that, those who had been driving for decades had much larger posterior hypocampi than those who had just begun. An extraordinary finding, really, that the brain can grow when exercised much as a muscle.

Had I known about neuronal plasticity many years ago, I could have informed Sister Martha that my inability to answer difficult multiplication problems was due to inadequate neuronal development in the left parietal lobe (an area involved in arithmetic abilities). But I did not, and such a response would likely have resulted in application of the ruler with some force to whatever part of the anatomy Sister Martha guessed housed my left parietal lobe. So, I suppose it is just as well that such knowledge has come to us only recently.

2

Changes in Memory
Across the
Adult Life Span

On January 29, 1986, the day after the tragic explosion of the space shuttle *Challenger,* an indelible memory for many of us, I attended a meeting of memory experts from around the world at the Casa Marina Resort in Key West, Florida. The topic was Age-Related Memory Loss and whether the magnitude of "normal" memory loss by age fifty and beyond was sufficient to merit treatment.

I was serving as Chairman of the meeting. Although I knew my position, debate raged back and forth on the issue. Slowly and tentatively, the door behind me opened and a gentleman appeared, dressed in a blue–and–white-striped seersucker suit and straw hat. Apparently in his mid-seventies, he entered the conference room. He appeared embarrassed at having entered and apologized, saying he had seen the title of the meeting on the door and wondered if it was open to the public. I indicated that the meeting was not open to the public, but I explained what it was about and asked his opinion about the topic being debated.

Here was an opportunity for the thirty or so outstanding memory scientists present to hear the view of "the man on the street." The gentleman gave a brilliant account of how his ability to learn and remember had declined slowly but dramatically over the years. He focused particularly on his ability to recall details of the lives of his friends and clients, saying that he could once remember the names of not only these individuals, but also names of spouses and children, their ages and minute details of their lives. This allowed him, his wife, and his secretary to respond to birthdays and anniversaries, as well as to special events and circumstances that would be unknown to people outside each individual's immediate family. He went on to say that he now often confused one family with another and one person's love of tennis for another's love of golf. He realized that he still had a remarkable store of knowledge about many hundreds and probably thousands of people, so he was scarcely on the edge of dementia, but he still felt that his fading memory posed serious problems in business and daily life.

Our unexpected visitor argued my view better than had any of the distinguished debaters: that "normal" age-related memory loss can severely interfere with daily function and is an appropriate condition to treat. Because I was (and remain) a proponent of treatment, I was jokingly accused by my colleagues of having hired an actor to make my case. In the same tone, I responded that, by accident, some of my distinguished colleagues had just been introduced to the real world.

Since that meeting twenty years ago, which marked the beginning of a serious effort to develop treatments for "normal' memory loss in later life, or "Age-Associated Memory Impairment" (AAMI) as it was designated by a National Institute of Mental Health (NIMH) Workgroup, I have seen thousands of adults who have come to our specialized memory clinics complaining of failing memory and seeking treatment. In most cases, these have been well-educated people who are in demanding intellectual roles. Even if retired, they may be avid readers, chess players, or may be engaged in other intellectual pursuits. However, they have noticed that some memory abilities are not what they were in high school or college.

Sometimes the concern is that they may be developing Alzheimer's disease (AD) or another dementing neurological illness. More often than not, though, they realize that memory loss is a normal consequence of aging and, nevertheless, they want to alter or reverse that process, if at all possible. Just as they exercise, diet, take medications or use expensive creams to alter the "normal" course of cardiovascular, musculoskeletal and dermatologic aging, so too are they intent on altering the "normal" course of brain aging.

This was not my grandparents' response to aging. I remember very well when my beloved grandparents, Raymond and Mary Hunter, were in their fifties, sixties, seventies and eighties. The idea of altering the normal course of body or brain aging would never have occurred to them. (This was, perhaps, not entirely true in the case of my grandmother because I do recall an odd, nocturnal facial mask ritual involving Pond's Cold Cream and, also, my grandmother's gray hair taking on a bluish purple hue that seemed to exist nowhere else in nature.) In general, my grandparents and virtually everyone else in their generation simply accepted loss of certain mental and physical capacities and gracefully moved on. Today, by contrast, in much of the developed world we see that what is "normal" is often not inevitable and we act accordingly.

I live and work in South Florida and have the opportunity to view, year round, the sometimes dramatic extent to which both men and women will go to maintain a youthful appearance. The "Yellow Pages" for the Fort Lauderdale area alone lists 118 individual or group cosmetic surgery practices, compared with only forty-eight general surgery practices. As the number of providers suggests, Botox and other treatments designed to reduce facial wrinkling are administered at parties given for that purpose. Gray hair has largely disappeared from large segments of the female population and, increasingly, segments of the older male population as well. Viagra and its competitors are extending the years of youthful male sexual performance. Most impressive to me, the wife of one of my friends, who is in her mid-fifties just returned from a Brazilian spa where the "exercise and diet" have, it would seem, done such wonders that she actually improved on her physique of thirty years ago. Both wife and husband are very pleased with the results.

But, returning to memory, what is "normal" age-related memory loss? When does it begin? Does it affect all types of memory? Does it affect everyone? Do doctors now recognize it as an appropriate condition to treat? Does it signal a risk for dementia? When should one worry that what he or she is experiencing is not normal? There is not universal agreement on any of these questions, but let's consider each.

What is "Normal" Age-Related Memory Loss?

Memory loss occurs with advancing age in every species of animal or insect that has been studied. This includes not only man, but various species of monkeys, dogs and cats, rats and mice, primitive sea snails—even fruit flies that have a life span of only fifteen days. Let's consider the very simple memory test illustrated below and compare how similar are the declines that occur in humans and in non-human primates—in this case, Cebus Monkeys.

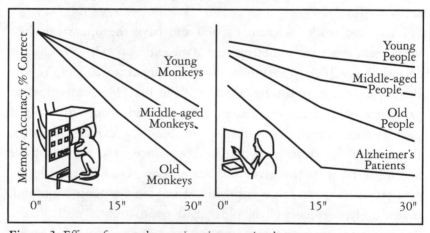

Figure 3. Effect of age and retention time on visual memory

In the test shown in Figure 3, developed by the distinguished neuroscientist Dr. Raymond T. Bartus, the subject, whether human or monkey, sits in front of a panel with an array of squares, each of which can be illuminated. The monkey panel has nine squares and the human panel has twenty-five, arranged as if they were rooms in a house. As each square is illuminated the testee, whether human or monkey, must reach out and touch it. The human is verbally rewarded for success and the monkey receives a banana-flavored pellet. After a few successful attempts, the test changes so that the testee cannot immediately touch the screen after the light goes off, but must remember which square was illuminated for a time (fifteen to thirty seconds). Both humans and monkeys of different ages were tested and, humans with moderate to severe dementia were tested as well. As you can see from the figure, the longer the time the testee must remember which square was lighted, the poorer was the performance of old monkeys compared with young. The same is true with humans, and it is not surprising that the memory loss was further exaggerated in subjects with dementia. So, on this test, age-related memory loss in monkeys is parallel to that seen in neurologically healthy humans.

This parallel between monkeys and humans may not be too surprising, or even the parallel between humans and rodents, demonstrated many hundreds of times. But you might find it more surprising that memory loss occurs with advancing age even in drosophila, a fruit fly with a life span of fifteen days. How do we know this? Well, drosophila can be trained to avoid particular odors by administering an electric shock when they approach an area of a glass enclosure saturated with that odor. Through such conditioning, early in life drosophila will scrupulously avoid that area. As they reach the last days of their life, however, they begin to forget the association and wander into areas with a particular scent previously associated with the aversive shock. Nearing the end of life, the association may be forgotten altogether.

There have been literally thousands of studies showing that older adults are less able than their young counterparts to learn and remember many types of information but, nevertheless, there is still controversy. You might even read about studies showing that memory does not decline with age. These different findings come about because, as we have already seen, there are different types of memory and they are differentially susceptible to the effects of aging and even dementia. Recall, for example, the discussion of procedural memory and the patient with AD, Frederick, who could remember the rules and terminology of golf, as well as select the proper club, and swing with skill, even though he would later have no recollection of having played just hours before.

At the other extreme, maximum decline occurs with age when new and unfamiliar information must be learned and recalled quickly. This is seen particularly in the presence of distraction and where no cues are available to assist recall. So, for example, a sixty-eight-year-old man is likely to have a great deal more difficulty than his eighteen-year-old counterpart when both are enrolled in a crash course to learn a new language or a complicated new technical skill. The older man's difficulty will be further exaggerated if the pace of teaching is rapid, there is no opportunity for solitary study, and there are no multiple choice questions on the exam.

By contrast, minimal or no memory decline occurs through the adult years when the information to be recalled was learned long ago and was continuously rehearsed over many years and where, in addition, there is no stringent time limit for recalling the information and recall cues are provided. For example, older adults are almost as able as their young counterparts to recall the meaning of vocabulary words learned years ago when there are generous time limits for recalling the information. When a multiple-choice format is employed, there is generally no difference between healthy old and young subjects on a test of this ability.

Most psychological tests used to assess learning and memory in research and in clinical practice are quite abstract and have little to do with the kinds of memory tasks we all face in daily life. That makes it difficult to understand the significance of most psychological studies of memory and aging. In the test below, for example, you are presented with six pairs of nonsense syllables. Find a blank piece of paper and a pen or pencil before you begin the test. Now, your task is to slowly read the six pairs aloud and try, as you read, to memorize which syllables are paired together. Now turn the page to where only one side of the list is presented and the words are in a different order. Place your paper next to the list and then try to write the nonsense syllable that corresponds to each of the syllables listed. Please complete the test before reading further.

AUG – ZAF

PEV – TIG

GOJ – JUV

WID – YAT

DUT – CIG

HOZ – MIP

PEV – _____

DUT – _____

AUG – _____

HOZ – _____

GOJ – _____

WID – _____

Very easy, wasn't it? If you are normal and have no memory problems, you probably got all the answers correct. Palms sweating? I'm just kidding. When one does memory research for thirty years one's comedic range is limited. This is an extremely difficult test and few of you will have gotten more than one or two correct. Zero or one correct is normal if you are a middle-aged or older adult and one or two correct is normal if you are a young adult. Call me if you got five or six correct and I'll try to convince you to donate your brain to science.

Because of the difficulty in extrapolating from abstract tests to everyday life, my colleagues and I launched an effort more than twenty years ago to develop a computerized test battery that relates directly to the memory problems we all face on a day-to-day basis. We were interested in studying the effects of various treatments in AAMI and we thought it would seem reasonable for the measure of a treatment's effects to have some relationship to the problems for which people seek treatment. This idea proved radical in some academic quarters where (think back to the gentleman in the seersucker suit in Key West) debate often centers on obscure concepts rather than real-life problems.

The first problem we had in developing a computerized test battery more than twenty years ago was that there weren't any proper computers, software, or peripheral equipment. Microsoft was not yet a public corporation and no one had heard of Bill Gates. We wanted to simulate real life problems on video and the greatest hard disk storage capacity we could get on a PC was 40 megabytes. Today I carry a two inch by 3/8 inch "memory stick" to lectures in my pocket that stores hundreds of slides, and enough live video to conduct all of our tests, with plenty of space left over. Fortunately, I found a brilliant young computer engineer, Bruce Johnson, and we constructed a test battery simulating everyday memory tasks using those early PCs, complicated and unreliable read-write laser disk players, 70 pound Sony visual monitors with hand crafted touchscreens, and various manipulanda interfaced with the computer. We created a telephone dialing task, for example, in which the subject was asked to dial telephone numbers that appeared briefly on the screen. In the most sadistic version of this test, the subject reads and then dials a ten-digit, long distance number, receives a busy signal and then must redial from memory.

In other examples, we had series of fourteen people appear individually on live video and introduce themselves. They then reappeared at varying intervals of time and subjects were asked to recall the name of each individual. On another test, we showed a computer representation of a house to subjects and then asked them to place representations of objects such as keys and eyeglasses (using a touch screen) in rooms where they could best be recalled later. Thirty minutes later they were shown the house again and asked to recall the location of each object by touching the room into which it had been placed earlier. In one test, subjects were presented with radio traffic and news broadcasts while performing a simulated driving task and later asked to recall the factual content of the broadcasts. Tests were intended for repeated administration, so there were eight separate versions of each test, all developed in six different languages. Therefore, a great deal of work went into test development. We developed an entire library of such tests and then proceeded to use them in many studies, including those examining the consequences in daily life of age-related memory loss.

We tested tens of thousands of healthy normal subjects, and even administered an Italian version of our tests in cities and small towns throughout that country to obtain a true random sample of the entire Italian population. We had a mobile clinic where subjects, as pictured on the next page, were tested and examined by neurologists and psychologists to be sure none was suffering from a disease that could affect memory.

Those of you who might be ever so slightly skeptical about the scientific purity of our motive might ask why the latter study to which I referred was performed in Italy rather than, say, North Dakota in February or Arizona in July. Such skepticism is always healthy, but in this case there's a pretty good answer.

First, let me step back and say that most studies that purport to establish what is "normal" at various ages do not study a true random sample of a large population. Rather, they study people of different ages within a "sample of convenience." This may be residents of the city where the study is conducted, university students, faculty, and retired faculty, and so on. Results of such studies can be quite misleading when applied to a much larger group, such as a national population, because the subjects studied differ from the larger group in terms of education, health or many other variables. This is also complicated because in America we migrate and sometimes migration is a function of mental ability. The brightest kids in small towns might migrate to big cities for greater economic opportunities; economically able retirees might migrate to Florida and Arizona and so on. Beyond that, because of socialized medicine, it is possible to go into any town in Italy, randomly select persons within different age groups and determine their address, phone number and other information necessary to contact them, and in that contact we would have the support of the town mayor and the local priest. Can you imagine how difficult it would be in the United States to identify people to test and then contact them later? It would be harder yet to convince people to come to our van parked on the local Wal-Mart parking lot to be tested. Finally, there is little migration in Italy, often two or even three generations live within the same home. Thus, it is much easier to conduct a random population study of aging and memory. So that's why we went to Italy to study memory and aging. The decision had almost nothing at all to do with the wonderful people and style of life, the ancient culture, or the incredible food and wine.

An important finding of the study was that normal healthy aged subjects were *much* less able than corresponding young adults to perform many (but not all) critical tasks of daily life. We had conducted a number of parallel studies in the U.S. and elsewhere in Europe but always in samples of convenience, as is the case with the vast majority of published work in psychology. We found such studies understate the extent of "normal" memory loss seen in the general population. For example, Figure 5 illustrates the decade by decade decline with age in the ability to remember the name of an individual to whom one is introduced, the memory task considered of greatest significance and considered most problematic

Figure 4. Italian mobile clinic and subject being tested

in every culture we have studied. You will note that by age sixty-five, subjects show a 62% deficit on this task, relative to age twenty-five, and by age seventy-five, the deficit has increased to 74%.

Now, the extent of memory decline is not the same on all of our memory tests. Some memory abilities are preserved as we age much better than others. For example, the ability to recognize someone you met previously is preserved much better than the ability to remember his name. It is very difficult to remember a long distance phone number long enough to dial when you are sixty-five (remember, this is working memory), but some people are occasionally able to do this. If you encounter a busy signal and have to redial from memory, you will have difficulty at any age and are very likely to fail if you are fifty years old or beyond.

Once again, bear in mind that all the subjects we studied in Italy were medically screened by physicians and psychologists in our mobile clinic to exclude those with conditions that might cause

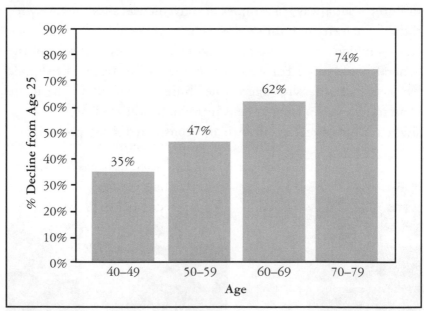

Figure 5. Decline in memory with advancing age when remembering names one hour after introduction

memory loss. If such people had not been excluded from the study, the deficit would be even greater because, as we shall see in the next chapter, many older adults have medical conditions, or must take drugs for medical conditions, that cause additional memory problems beyond these "normal" deficits.

When Does Age-Related Memory Loss Begin?

One does not awaken on one's fiftieth, sixtieth or eightieth birthday with memory problems that did not exist the night before. If you again examine Figure 5, for example, you will see that, in recalling names of persons to whom one is introduced, as early as age forty-five there is a 35% loss relative to age twenty-five. Of course, there are many types of memory and, as in sports, one reaches peak performance on different tasks at different ages. A female gymnast might reach peak performance at age fourteen or fifteen while a male discus hurler may perform at Olympic levels until almost age fifty. Similarly, in the domain of learning and memory, the ability to acquire a new language may peak in early childhood while the ability to combine and gain insight into much that lies in semantic memory may peak in the latest decades of life. But it is apparent from our studies that on many critical tasks that we must all perform in daily life—from remembering names to remembering what we just read in a newspaper or where we put our eyeglasses—a significant decline begins quite early in life, often in the late thirties and early forties. It is noteworthy too that there is almost as much distress about age-related memory loss among persons in their thirties as among those three and four decades older. As shown in Figure 6 on the next page, there is no clear relation between age and concern that one has experienced age-related memory loss.

I cannot tell you how many people in their thirties, often early thirties, I have seen for evaluation because they think they are losing their edge. In fact, they may be correct if they are operating in very demanding, often stressful situations—trading commodity

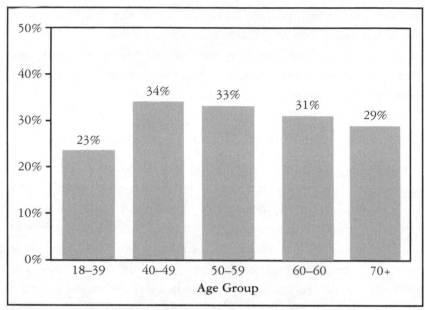

Figure 6. Percent of people who report that their memory is "much worse than the best it has ever been"

futures on the floor of the Chicago Mercantile Exchange, for example. They may be performing in the top one-tenth of one percent of the population or higher, but are still not at the level they operated a decade earlier. Often they can compensate for this by the wisdom learned on the job, but the combination of that wisdom with the speed of memory abilities they had in earlier years would be incredible.

Are All Types of Memory Affected?

Deficits associated with aging are limited primarily to declarative memory. The old saw about never forgetting how to ride a bike is largely true, as procedural memory is generally spared in the course of normal aging. One would hope, of course, that procedural memory of how to ride a bike would be accompanied by intact episodic memories of the possible hazards of doing so. Both short-term and remote memory are not spared entirely in normal aging, but deficits are comparatively modest.

It is interesting, by the way, that some information held in remote memory, about which the individual is absolutely certain, may, in fact, be discovered to be erroneous when verification is possible. There are only a few studies in which investigators went to a great deal of effort in attempting to validate the memories of older adults of events that occurred decades ago, and they suggest that such memories are often not consistent with discoverable facts or memories of others who were present. As we shall see in coming chapters, however, that this is not necessarily a bad thing. Most of us distort memories that are not consistent with our self-image and, if one's self-image is positive, such distortions are often healthy.

Is Everyone Affected?

Figure 7 illustrates the number of individuals at each decade who meet diagnostic criteria for *Age-Associated Memory Impairment* (AAMI), the diagnostic term for normal, age-related memory loss adopted at the meeting that I mentioned occurred in Key West twenty years ago. It describes people at least fifty years of age who complain that their memory has declined since high school or college, and who score significantly lower on neuropsychological memory tests than do young adults. They must, however, score within the range of normality for their age and show no clinical evidence of dementia. To be included in this diagnostic category, one must be free of the many psychiatric and medical conditions which could be the cause of the memory loss they have experienced. As you can see, few individuals can expect to be spared. As shown in Figures 7 and 8, these prevalence figures are comparable to figures for far-sightedness (Presbyopia) and other age-related degenerative conditions where the prevalence by age fifty is essentially 100%. This is not to say that one cannot stave off age-related memory loss for a time and mitigate its effects, indeed we will argue later in the

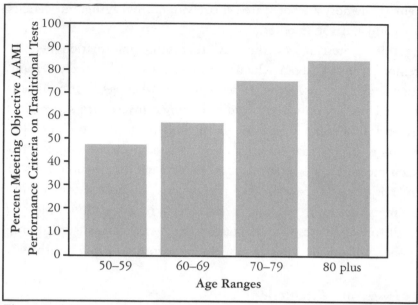

Figure 7. AAMI prevalence estimated from standard clinical memory tests

book that this is certainly possible. I point out here similarities between the effects of aging on brain and other organ systems, but I also want to emphasize that a forty year old athlete in most sports will be a pale shadow of what he was at twenty, while a seventy-year-old intellectual can regard his juniors of fifty years as promising upstarts.

Do Physicians Regard AAMI as an Appropriate Condition to Treat?

Both the American Psychiatric Association and the American Psychological association have accepted AAMI, also referred to as *Age-Related Cognitive Decline* (ARCD), in their diagnostic systems as conditions that "merit attention and treatment," although there are at this time no drugs approved by the American Food and Drug Administration (FDA) to treat the condition. There are four drugs on the American market for Alzheimer's disease and at least

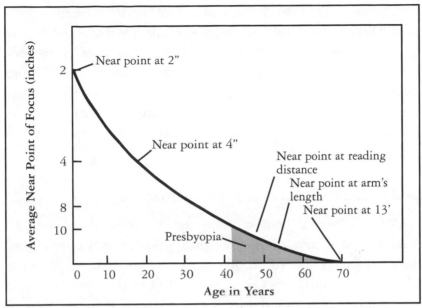

Figure 8. Relationship between age and presbyopia

two of these have therapeutic effects in AAMI, but the modest magnitude of effects and the presence of side-effects would preclude their use by physicians in AAMI. My colleagues and I have studied many potential drug treatments for AAMI and have found effective compounds, but no drugs that meet the rigid safety requirements rightfully imposed by the FDA. In Chapter 5, we discuss supplements that do not require a prescription and have been found effective.

Although many physicians have not yet accepted the idea of treating normal age-related memory loss, this attitude is fading in an era where treatment for "normal" age-related loss of bone mass and hormone replacement therapy is routine in post-menopausal women; Viagra is routinely prescribed for "erectile dysfunction," a diagnosis that applies to most males over fifty; and Botox is approved by the FDA to reduce normal age-related facial "frown lines" and is used much more broadly to maintain a youthful appearance.

We must bear in mind, too, that AAMI is not a cosmetic condition. There are very real consequences in the workplace and in performing other demanding intellectual and social tasks. If memory and learning deficits of the same magnitude seen in AAMI were seen in an adolescents or young adult, there is little question that the problem would be taken quite seriously and treated. So, one could ask why the same deficit in an older adult would be less deserving of treatment.

Is AAMI a Risk Factor for Dementia?

AAMI is a "normal" phenomenon and is not associated with an increased risk of developing Alzheimer's disease or other dementing disorders. As mentioned previously, persons are excluded from the diagnosis of AAMI if they score below the expected range for their age on neuropsychological tests of memory or show any evidence of dementia. *Mild Cognitive Impairment* (MCI) is the diagnostic category used to describe people who are not demented, but who score below the expected range *for their age* on neuropsychological memory tests, and who show evidence on clinical interview that memory loss is having an effect on their ability to function at home or in the workplace. MCI is associated with an increased risk of developing Alzheimer's disease or another dementing disorder and the rate of conversion may be on the order of 15%–20% per year. The four drugs approved to treat Alzheimer's disease in the United States are being studied in MCI, with mixed results so far.

When Should I Worry That Memory Loss Is Not Normal?

In general, if memory problems are affecting your ability, or that of a loved one, to perform normal duties at home or at work, consultation with your physician or a psychologist may be in order. Problems misplacing keys, forgetting names after introduction, or forgetting the dry cleaning are probably normal, while forgetting familiar names, becoming lost when driving a familiar route, or forgetting that you had dinner at the neighbor's house two days ago may not be. I recall one patient who was finally forced to confront his memory problems when he took his wife out to dinner, went out afterward to retrieve the car, forgot his wife was waiting and drove home alone. Only after his wife called home did he realize he had forgotten her. This is the sort of problem that may reflect either a serious memory or marital problem. As you will see in the next chapter, there are many causes of memory loss other than aging and each of these can be evaluated by a trained professional.

Keep in mind too that there is a poor correlation between one's self evaluation of memory and actual objective performance on memory tests. I have seen many people with Alzheimer's disease who tell me they have no memory problem at all. They are quite capable of dealing with questions such as "How are you feeling?" or "Nice day today, isn't it?" but they are often unaware of where they are or what month or year it is. They often can't name the president of the United States, and yet they maintain their memory is fine and they have come to the clinic only to mollify their spouse or an adult child. On the other hand, I have seen many people who are convinced they have Alzheimer's disease and yet score in a perfectly normal or even superior range on memory testing. Often these latter patients are depressed and may remain convinced that they are on the road to a nursing home even after being assured that their test results are normal. A depressed person may tell you that his memory is seriously failing but, upon broader questioning, he will also tell you that he is unhappy with his spouse and his job, his health is failing, he has no energy, has no interest in friends and he feels sad and blue.

In Appendix 1 of this book we provide several tests that you might find useful. The First–Last Names Association Test, which my colleagues and I developed, allows you to compare your performance to both other people your age and to young adults who are performing optimally. This allows you to determine whether your performance falls within the bounds of AAMI or whether you actually perform better than others your age. Please bear in mind that these are only two tests and a much more sophisticated neuropsychological battery would be administered in the clinic to make diagnostic decisions about your memory.

In Appendix 2 we provide the most widely used instrument, the Mini-Mental Status Examination (MMSE) developed by Drs. Folstein, Folstein and McHugh, to screen for dementing disorders such as Alzheimer's disease. No matter what you have read, there is no definitive diagnostic procedure for Alzheimer's disease until the brain can be examined after death and, even then, the diagnosis is often equivocal. You may find the MMSE of value in determining if a problem exists (it obviously should not be self-administered) but do not let a satisfactory score override your judgment if you see problems caused by memory in daily life.

3

Causes of Memory Problems at Any Age

Over the years, my colleagues and I have seen many people of all ages who complain that their ability to learn and remember new information, to concentrate, or to think clearly has been greatly, and sometimes suddenly, diminished. These men and women who come to consult with my colleagues and with me are often in a panicked state, afraid that they may have Alzheimer's disease or some other neurological or medical disorder with a grim prognosis.

A sudden decline is not typical of age-related memory loss where, as we have seen, the hallmark is a gradual decline over the course of decades. In a sudden degeneration, sometimes the problem can be attributed to a single event—head trauma, for example—and sometimes there is no obvious problem associated with the cognitive symptoms. However, it's best to begin cases like these with a detailed neuropsychological and medical evaluation. Such investigations sometimes take us in unexpected directions, as the following example illustrates.

Morris was a fifty-eight-year-old engineer. He came to me because he had been experiencing memory loss and had difficulty concentrating. Morris also complained of feeling down, and of having generalized fatigue. Neuropsychological testing was consistent with AAMI. There was no evidence of focal brain lesions on neuropsychological testing or on a Computerized Axial Tomography (CAT) brain scan. His height was five feet eight inches, and he weighed 214 pounds. Suffering from moderate hypertension, Morris was already prescribed an antihypertensive drug (Capoten) and a diuretic. He indicated that he'd stopped smoking cigarettes two years earlier, following the diagnosis of lung cancer and subsequent death of an older brother. His cognitive problems and fatigue also began around that time and had continuously worsened since.

Morris had gained more than fifty pounds since he stopped smoking and attributed his fatigue and depressed feelings to the weight gain. Morris and his wife were interviewed about his health and lifestyle to see if there might be other factors that could account for the memory loss. A portion of the standardized interview focused on sleep habits, and Morris was asked about sleep onset, awakenings and duration of sleep. When his wife was asked to verify the information Morris provided, she said she had no idea if the information was correct because she slept in what had been the bedroom of one of the now adult children at the opposite end of the house. It seemed Morris had always snored loudly and the problem had worsened. She could no longer get a good night's sleep in the same room. Here we had our first clear clue as to what might be responsible for the Morris' memory loss and fatigue.

A condition known as *sleep apnea* is marked by cessation of breathing during the night. It's characterized by loud snoring and gasping and can greatly reduce oxygen delivery to the brain. Each period of breathing cessation lasts ten seconds or more and dozens or even hundreds of these episodes can occur during the course of one night, thus producing symptoms of both memory loss and fatigue the following day. It's a common problem for overweight individuals. Referral to a specialist confirmed Morris' diagnosis of *Obstructive*

Sleep Apnea. A neurologist prescribed a rather uncomfortable device temporarily to keep the airway open, and established an aggressive weight loss and exercise program for Morris.

We saw Morris again after six and twelve months of treatment. By the latter date, Morris performed much better on memory tests. He had lost thirty-seven pounds and had become a semi-avid jogger. Snoring was a greatly diminished problem. Morris's wife was gradually working her way back into their old bedroom and his memory problems were all but forgotten.

When memory problems develop suddenly, or are rapidly exacerbated, many factors must be considered. In this chapter, we'll consider some of the most frequently seen causes of these problems.

Drugs

It's true that illicit drugs taken by Baby Boomers years ago might present memory problems decades later. However, a far greater problem these days is the side effects of drugs prescribed for the full range of medical and psychiatric disorders.

Even such common household remedies as cough syrups and antihistamines can be potentially problematic for learning and memory. A wide range of these products contain sedating drugs such as diphenhydramine (for example, Benadryl). Memory loss is also associated with many drugs prescribed to treat anxiety or for sleep disorders. Some of these drugs, including benzodiazepines related to Valium and Librium, are even used in anesthetic regimens during surgery because their amnesic effects for the pain and discomfort of surgery might be considered adaptive.

Even though I have studied benzodiazepines and reported on their amnesic effects, I was amazed when I had two minor surgical procedures and a benzodiazepine was used in the witch's brew concocted by the anesthesiologist. The first time, more than twenty years ago, I was operated on for a sports injury and the drug lorazepam was used intravenously. After being administered the drug, I remember looking up at my nurse and feeling a tremendous sense of relief. My anxiety about the operation just lifted away. Suddenly, I understood why people use these drugs for sleep and anxiety. The effect was much more profound than I expected. I also remembered waking up groggy an hour or so after the operation and having had absolutely no recollection of what happened, even though I apparently talked, answered questions, and remained awake during the entire procedure. More recently, about two years ago, I had hand surgery and was again amazed at the same phenomenon. This time, however, a newer drug (Versed) in the same class was used, and this drug was much faster and shorter acting. I literally got off the operating table feeling almost fully alert, and walked away without assistance. Still, I have had no memory of the operation, even though I was conscious the entire time.

Among the most problematic and common drugs that may impair memory are those that block the neurotransmitter acetylcholine (pronounced: a see til kō leen). As you may recall from the first chapter, neurotransmitters are chemicals in your brain that facilitate the passage of electrical signals from one neuron to another. Acetylcholine is a neurotransmitter of critical importance for memory. Drugs that block or degrade this neurotransmitter are said to have anticholinergic effects. We have known for more than thirty years that some of these anticholinergic drugs (such as scopolamine, used in lower doses in a patch for seasickness), can produce memory loss so profound as to resemble dementia when administered to healthy young adults. (Don't worry, though: the effects wear off in an hour or two and are immediately reversible with drugs that elevate acetylcholine levels).

Brain acetylcholine levels decline with age and in those suffering from Alzheimer's disease (AD). Three of the four drugs approved by the FDA in the United States to treat AD do so by elevating brain acetylcholine levels. Because brain acetylcholinergic depletion occurs as a function of normal aging, older adults are particularly susceptible to the memory-impairing effects of anticholinergic drugs. Also, anticholinergic effects are additive, and older adults may be taking several drugs with anticholinergic effects, thus causing memory problems far greater than those associated with a single drug. A list of the anti-cholinergic drugs most commonly prescribed to older adults is provided in Figure 9.

Take a look at the medications you are taking and examine with your doctor the possible effects of each on learning and memory.

Also, if you are taking more than one prescription drug, it's important that you consult with your physician about how the combination of drug regimens might have unusual or different side effects. Take an inventory of your medicine cabinet, then have a talk with your doctor.

Anticholinergic Drugs and Drugs with Anticholinergic Side Effects Used in the Elderly

Anticholinergics

- Antiemetics/antivertigo
- Anti-Parkinson's
- Antispasmodics
- Antimigraines
- Bronchodilators
- Pre-anesthetics
- Mydriatics

Drugs with anticholinergic side effects

- Antiarrhythmics
- Antidiarrheals
- Antihistamines
- Skeletal muscle relaxants
- Antiulcer drugs
- Antidepressants
- Antipsychotics

Figure 9. Anticholinergic drugs and drugs with anticholinergic side effects

My colleagues and I have seen so many cases in which memory has improved—sometimes dramatically—when anticholinergic drugs have been discontinued. I'm not advocating the discontinuation of use of these drugs if they're needed. Again, it's a matter to discuss with your physician. There may not be an alternative in achieving medical efficacy. However, in some cases, a drug may be readily available with no significant anticholinergic effects and equal medical efficacy.

For example, we found that, among antidepressants similar in efficacy, sertraline (Zoloft), a very common selective serotonin reuptake inhibitor, produces no memory problems while amytripyline (Elavil), a potent anticholinergic tricyclic antidepressant, produces profound problems on such everyday memory tasks as remembering names or what one just read in a newspaper. Similarly, among equally efficacious drugs prescribed for *over active bladder syndrome* (OAB), oxybutynin (Ditropan), a powerful anticholinergic, produces highly significant memory problems while darifenacin (Enablex) does not. Both drugs are equally effective for such symptoms of OAB as urinary urge and incontinence.

Stress

It's just a reality. Modern life is stressful. Just getting the kids out the door before you rush off to a rough day at the office is enough to strain anybody's brain. You might be surprised to learn that while you're patiently, quietly, getting done what needs to be done—day in, day out—profound chemical reactions, triggered in the brain, are occurring throughout your body.

There's a normal hormonal response to stress in which the hypothalamus, a part of the limbic system at the base of the brain that's critical in regulating many body functions, releases a hormone, corticotrophin releasing factor (CRF). This travels a short distance to the anterior pituitary gland where another hormone, adrenocorticotrophic hormone (ACTH), is released and travels via the bloodstream to the adrenal glands that sit above the kidneys. This stimulates the production and releases yet another hormone, cortisol. This hormone largely controls your body's reactions to stress. And what does your body do when you're quietly (or not so quietly) panicking? Blood glucose levels rise and your blood pressure may sky-rocket. Also, the production of other crucial hor-

mones and amino acids can be inhibited, including those that provide feedback to the hypothalamus to stop producing CRF. So a
vicious circle can begin, producing prolonged physiological
effects that are not adaptive.

A normal stress response might improve mental performance in
the short run. However, during prolonged stress, cortisol and the
other stress hormones can impair verbal declarative and spatial
memory. They can also lead to cell loss and shrinkage in the hippocampus. This may be due, in part, to a decrease in brain glucose,
as glucose is directed to muscle tissues and blood vessels critical in
bodily defense. In his brilliant book *Why Zebras Don't Get Ulcers,*
Robert Sapolsky argues that humans are not programmed to deal
with prolonged stress and that its effects are often physically and
mentally deleterious.

There are many ways to deal with stress, as discussed in Dr.
Sapolsky's book. If stress is a serious problem for you, pick techniques to reduce it that fit your lifestyle and identity. Yoga and
other means of meditation are wonderfully effective for certain people, but it may be that watching a football game with your buddies
is the optimal stress remedy for you. Find out what works best for
you. Whatever it takes, making a serious, concerted effort to reduce
stress in your life will produce incredible results. Jogging ten miles
is great for many of my friends, but relaxing on the sofa with a good
book and their favorite music is ideal for others. What's important
is that you develop non-destructive ways of dealing with the immediate stressor (deep breathing, count to ten, etc.). Often, even more
important is that you develop methods of taking your mind off the
office, the household bills, your relationship with your spouse, the
pathetic state of your retirement account, or whatever else is causing you chronic stress.

Some of these sources of stress will have been exaggerated in
your mind and will disappear on their own when your attention is
elsewhere. Others will require your attention, but Step One in
addressing them is to relax, compose yourself and approach the

problem at the appropriate time with all your cognitive abilities optimally performing.

Many of you have been in extraordinary stressful situations where your body takes over for you and releases endogenous anti-stress hormones, likely including endogenous opioids. It's certainly happened to me. In the heat of battle, some combat veterans have later reported they felt a sense of peace, a feeling of well-being and a sense that everything was happening in slow motion. This is said to occur even though they had been under great stress, and felt quite anxious in the days and hours preceding the battle. I suspect that many of you who have never been in combat have had similar experiences when in an extremely stressful situation. In my case, I remember, as a teenager, being with my father in a small boat that sank as we were testing it in the Chesapeake Bay. Unfortunately, we had no life preservers aboard (my father was not generally a prudent man) and it was March. The water was so cold that muscles contracted and cramped immediately. Swimming a few miles to shore was impossible. I remember my heart pounding and feeling very anxious as we tried to save the boat, but when it disappeared under the waves, I felt a great sense of peace and that everything after that occurred in slow motion. We were eventually rescued by the only boat within many miles, which had not been initially visible to us. In a remarkable navigational feat, the captain and crew of a tugboat saw objects from the boat floating many miles from us and judged by the winds and tide the course that the objects had come from.

Perhaps these anti-stress hormones are also released very near death, and produce the feeling of peace and perception of light that is so frequently reported by people who have had near-death experiences. Of course, some will find explanations for rescue boats that appear out of nowhere, or light and peace at death that lie beyond science.

Of course, we cannot count on endogenous anti-stress hormones very often, and for those of you interested in stress reduction techniques in greater detail, we have provided in Appendix 4 a description of techniques I have found effective over the years. Beyond that, there is Dr. Sapolsky's book and many other, perfectly fine books on stress reduction.

Cardiovascular Health

Heart disease kills more Americans than any other disease, including cancer. The American Heart Association estimates that over sixty-one million Americans have cardiovascular disease. A million die from it every year. But can having a healthy heart help you remember where you put your keys? You bet. A fully healthy body that is functioning optimally allows you to perform at your best, mentally and emotionally

When considering the relationship between cardiovascular health and cognitive abilities, most people think of stroke. Indeed, each year in the United States more than three million people suffer a serious stroke. These events can produce profound impairment of memory and other cognitive and motor abilities.

As you will recall from Chapter 1, certain areas of the brain control certain cognitive and motor abilities, so the effects of a stroke will in part depend upon where in the brain the event occurs. For example, in the most general sense, a stroke in the left cerebral hemisphere is likely to produce paralysis or other functional impairments on the right side of the body. This may also mean impairments of verbal function and analytical reasoning, which are largely localized in the left cerebral cortex. By contrast, a right hemisphere stroke may produce motor impairments on the left side of the body and impairments on visual spatial and creative abilities localized largely in the right hemisphere.

The most common type of stroke is *ischemic stroke,* which occurs when a blood clot or other blockage forms in an artery leading to the brain. This accounts for almost eighty percent of all strokes. An *intracerebral hemorrhage,* by contrast, is caused by a sudden rupture of an artery within the brain and the subsequent compression of brain structures caused by blood within the brain. A *subarachnoid hemor-rhage* is also caused by the sudden rupture of an artery but, in this case, the rupture leads to blood entering the space around the brain rather than the brain itself.

In a stroke, brain damage is sudden and localized. Many cognitive and motor abilities may be recovered in subsequent rehabilitation. In dementia, by contrast, onset is generally slow and the loss of memory and other cognitive abilities is unrelenting. Several decades ago, it was believed that the most common cause of dementia was cerebrovascular disease and the term Alzheimer's disease was restricted to those rare cases in which dementia developed quite early in life, generally in one's forties and fifties. Terminology changed during the 1970s when it was discovered, on autopsy, that the same changes in the brain seen in early onset dementia patients (basically deposition of a sticky amyloid plaque and tangled neuronal structures in brain areas critical for memory) were also seen in the majority of patients with disease onset in their seventies, eighties and beyond.

The diagnostic term *Alzheimer's disease* then came to be applied to those patients who became demented without evidence of cerebrovascular disease or other causative factors. AD is, thus, a diagnosis of exclusion that can only be confirmed on autopsy, and even then, coexisting cerebrovascular problems are common. *Vascular dementia,* generally with evidence of stroke and other lesions visible on neuroradiologic scan, is a diagnosis used to describe fewer than twenty percent of elderly patients with dementia in the United States and Europe, but approximately fifty percent in Japan. The greater prevalence in Japan is probably reflective of higher sodium intake in Japan and other dietary differences, as well as greater attention to cardiovascular health in the U.S. and other cultural factors. It is probably not genetic because Japanese-Americans have a much higher probability of developing AD relative to vascular dementia than do Japanese remaining in their mother country.

We seem to be moving away from the view that cardiovascular factors play only a secondary role in the majority of cases of dementia. It's increasingly apparent that cardiovascular health is also of major significance in Alzheimer's disease. For example, a recent study suggests that regular exercise may delay the onset of AD. This supports several earlier studies of thousands of patients that came to that same conclusion.

Aside from stroke and dementia, there is a condition sometimes referred to as *mild vascular cognitive impairment* (MCVI). This is comparable to the diagnosis of Mild Cognitive Impairment (MCI) referred to in the last chapter. In both cases, older subjects perform more poorly on memory and other tasks than would be expected for their age, in contrast to AAMI, but in MCVI, subjects have hypertension and other cardiovascular symptoms that suggests the cognitive loss is of vascular etiology.

How else might heart health impact your memory? Prolonged hypertension, myocardial infarction, congestive heart failure, cardiac insufficiency, and all conditions that lead to diminished oxygen delivery to the brain and consequent hypoxia, can produce memory and other cognitive problems. More than a half million coronary artery bypass graft surgeries are performed in the United States each year. This procedure alone may be associated with both short- and long-term memory problems.

Many cardiovascular problems can produce memory loss and other cognitive symptoms. However, the good news is that the vast majority of these cardiovascular problems are preventable or modifiable until quite late in life.

So how does one go about getting one's heart (and brain) in shape? Steps to prevent cardiovascular and subsequent cognitive problems are familiar to many, yet they bear repeating. If your goal is optimal health and brain function, read carefully through the following and evaluate whether you are doing all you can to achieve it.

Maintain appropriate body weight and lower elevated cholesterol and lipids. This will involve an appropriate diet low in saturated fats and high in fruits, vegetables and low-fat sources of pro-tein. Portion control and reduced carbohydrate intake will be appropriate for most people. Remember a pound of body weight is generally equivalent to 3,500 calories and that two Big Macs, a large McDonald's French fries and a large Coke are equal to half that number of calories and 75 delicious, but heart-clogging grams of fat. By contrast, my nightly 90-minute, 25-mile stationary bike ride at moderate elevation burns just under 600 calories and each one is painful. My point? It's easier to limit weight by reducing food intake than it is by burning excess calories. To control your cholesterol levels, it may also be necessary to take a statin such as atorvastatin (Lipitor), but that's a matter to discuss with your physician. Still, wouldn't you rather eat a healthy diet and avoid more prescription drugs with their myriad side effects?

Exercise! I recommend both resistance exercises with weights, three times per week if possible, and aerobics, six times per week if possible. If that's not possible, it's clear that even fifteen to twenty minutes of walking, three times per week is healthy for your heart and brain. Still, vigorous aerobic exercise is ideal for your heart, your brain and for stress reduction. In my experience, the best way to convert prolonged aerobic exercise into a tolerable experience is to reward yourself during exercise with something you enjoy. For example, I read historical adventure novels of absolutely no relevance to psychology or neuroscience during my ninety minute, nightly stationary bike rides and do not allow myself this luxury unless I am riding. As I am writing now, I cannot wait until 6:00 pm rolls around so I can get on the bike and see how Richard Sharpe, the hero of the novel I'm now reading, will emerge from his present very dire situation to, with just a little help from the Duke of Wellington, defeat the entire French Army at Waterloo. It's certainly possible to transform exercise from drudgery to something you enjoy.

Control hypertension. Both of the previous steps will help lower blood pressure, but if they are not adequate you must seek the advice of your physician in controlling even marginal hypertension. Bear in mind that hypertension is the number one predictor of stroke and vascular dementia and is, in itself, a detrimental factor in memory performance. Also, drugs may not be the answer. Many of the early anti-hypertensive drugs had problematic side effects. However, we have found that angiotensin converting enzyme inhibitors such as Capoten actually have positive effects on multiple aspects of psychological performance.

Control blood glucose levels. Diabetes is a huge and growing problem in this country. High blood glucose levels can damage the brain, impair memory and increase the risk of stroke and vascular dementia. Are you doing all you can to avoid becoming yet another statistic in this alarming and deadly epidemic?

Speak to your doctor or seek a second opinion to be sure that existing heart diseases including atrial fibrillation, congestive heart failure or diseases of the heart valves are being appropriately treated.

Eat (a baby) aspirin. Even if you have no existing heart disease you should be aware that there is a large and growing body of evidence that a "baby aspirin" (81 mg) per day can be of very significant value in preventing heart attack and stroke.

Stop smoking. If you're a smoker, you are now groaning. You know it's rotten, but you just can't quit. Believe me, whatever it takes to quit, it will be worth it. Half of those who continue to smoke all their lives die of the habit. Is that pleasurable puff really worth the risk you're taking with your health and your family's welfare? Smoking is risk factor for heart attack and stroke. But back to memory: smoking may also due direct damage to the brain by decreasing oxygen delivery

A glass of wine. One or two ounces of alcohol per day may be harmless or even beneficial to the heart and brain. Greater intake is a risk factor for stroke and may damage the brain directly.

Get enough sleep. An adequate amount of sleep each night allows your brain, heart and all organs of your body to slow down, relax and recharge before meeting the demands of the next day. You know that a good night's sleep improves your physical and mental performance the following day. If you want your brain to operate optimally, let those batteries charge. Useful tips in getting a good night's sleep are provided in Appendix 5.

Remember, excellent evidence is emerging of a close and direct relationship between a healthy heart and a healthy brain.

General Medical Health

Aside from cardiovascular disease, a number of medical conditions are associated with memory problems. Each should be considered before one concludes that memory loss is associated with aging or neurological diseases such as AD. A brief review of medical conditions that can cause memory loss is as follows:

Hypothyroidism

In my experience, one of the most important factors to consider when examining an individual with memory loss, particularly an older woman, is hypothyroidism. Approximately ten percent of women over sixty-five have clinical hypothyroidism and among substantially older women the prevalence may reach twenty percent or more. Among older diabetics, the condition may be expected among more than one-third of the population. The thyroid is a butterfly-shaped gland in the front of the neck, on either side of the Adam's Apple. It is under the control of the hypothalamus, in the base of the brain. In this case, the hypothalamus sends thyrotropin releasing hormone (TRH) to the adjacent anterior pituitary gland, which then sends thyroid stimulating hormone (TSH) to the thyroid gland which produces the thyroid hormones thyroxine (T4) and triodothyronine (T3). These hormones then travel to specific receptors in every cell in the body, including the brain, and control the rate of metabolism and all the physical and chemical processes that allow growth and maintain body function. Any problem along this route, or damage to the thyroid gland itself, can produce inadequate levels of thyroid hormones, referred to as hypothyroidism. There is substantial evidence that thyroid hormones influence memory. Decreased levels of T4 correspond with decreased cognitive performance and decreased levels TSH are associated with decreased episodic memory performance in healthy older adults. Even thyroid hormone levels in the low range of what is considered normal can produce memory problems. The problem is easily treated with drugs such as Synthroid (levothyroxine) which is a synthetic form of T4, so it is a shame when hypothyroid function goes unnoticed and symptoms ranging from memory loss to fatigue and impaired lipid metabolism exist unnecessarily. When hypothyroid function is properly treated, it can be very gratifying for patients, their family members and clinicians to see the dramatic improvement in memory and other symptoms that can occur.

Type 2 (non insulin-dependent) Diabetes and Insulin Resistance

Until about age sixty-five, there is not a highly significant difference between the cognitive performance of patients with Type 2 Diabetes and non-diabetics of the same age. After age sixty-five, Type 2 diabetics perform at a lower level on cognitive tests than do non-diabetics. This difference becomes exaggerated as age increases. It is almost as if diabetes speeds up the normal process of brain aging. Beyond this observation, there is substantial evidence, developed by Suzanne Craft at the University of Washington and others, that insulin is very important in normal memory processes and that, although acute doses of insulin can improve memory, chronic high levels of insulin do the opposite: they impair memory. Dr. Craft has shown that insulin affects levels of neurotransmitters in the brain such as acetylcholine that are critical in memory, as discussed earlier. It also affects glucose utilization in specific areas of the brain critical to memory. Dr. Craft has also demonstrated that insulin resistance can impair memory and that treatment of insulin resistance with drugs such as rosiglitazone (Avandia) can improve memory.

Estrogen and Testosterone Levels

Once again, this is a case in which releasing factors from the hypothalamus—in this case, gonadotropin-releasing hormone (Gn-RH) —travel the very short distance to the anterior pituitary gland where follicle-stimulating hormone (FSH) and luteinizing hormone (LH) are released. They then travel to the testes in males or the uterus in females to stimulate the production and release of estrogen, progesterone and testosterone. These hormones play important roles in memory and have direct effects in the hippocampus. Of course, levels of these hormones fluctuate on a monthly basis in pre-menopausal women, and they may fluctuate dramatically with pregnancy and childbirth. They are diminished in women very significantly at menopause. Testosterone levels also drop significantly in males, generally between ages fifty and sixty.

The importance of these changes in AAMI and AD, particularly among women, has been the subject of a heated debate for at least a decade. There have been studies showing improved memory among post-menopausal women given estrogen or estrogen and progesterone and studies showing that these treatments reduce the risk of AD. However, the recently completed Women's Health Initiative Memory Study (WHIMS) sponsored by the National Institutes of Health (NIH) was very large and well designed, and it showed a significant increase in the rate of onset of AD and a decrease in cognitive performance among women treated with estrogen alone or estrogen combined with progesterone. Critics note that the estrogen studied was derived from the urine of pregnant mares, and although this is by far the most common product (Prempro) sold for hormone replacement therapy in the United States, they argue that a phytoestrogen (derived from soy, for example) would not have produced these effects.

The bottom line at this point seems to be that if particularly low levels of estrogen or testosterone are seen in examining a patient with memory loss, this may be a causative factor, but the risks of treating with hormone replacement therapy (HRT), particularly for an extended period of time and particularly with testosterone, should be carefully weighed. Bear in mind that WHIMS also found increased risks of breast cancer, heart disease and blood clotting in women on HRT.

Also controversial is the association of pregnancy and childbirth with memory and other cognitive problems. Studies on the subject have generally been limited in their scientific value, but I have seen many women over the years who complain of significant memory loss and confusion during pregnancy or just after childbirth. A book due out this year from Cathryn Jacobson–Ramin, *Carved in Sand,* will explore this phenomenon in detail.

For now, the best course is a thorough evaluation of women with such complaints to assure there is not another causative factor and reassurance that, in the great majority of these cases, the problem is transitory and will be resolved without treatment.

Surgery and Anesthesia

I mentioned previously that coronary artery bypass graft procedures may produce both temporary and long-lasting memory problems. It now appears that other extended surgical procedures, at least in older adults, may also produce such problems. For example, hip replacement surgery has recently been associated with cognitive problems. Whether these problems are associated with hypoxia, with toxic effects of anesthesia, with immune function, or other factors is unknown. However, in my opinion, prior to surgery, a compound with neuroprotective effects, one of which will be described in Chapter 6, is worth discussing with your physician.

Cancer and Chemotherapy

Even cancers that have not invaded the central nervous system can have an adverse effect on cognition because of adverse effects on the immune and endocrine systems. Beyond that, it's becoming quite clear that chemotherapy can damage memory and other cognitive abilities, even to the extent that the unfortunate term "Chemo Brain" has been coined. Again, a compound with neuroprotective effects should be discussed with your physician prior to initiation of chemotherapy.

Other Medical Conditions

Many other medical conditions, ranging from infections to toxins, can cause memory loss and an encyclopedic listing is beyond the scope of this text. However, what's quite clear is that a comprehensive physical examination is called for when evaluating and individual who is found on neuropsychological evaluation to suffer from memory loss.

Neuropsychiatric Health

Two possible neuropsychiatric factors in memory loss that are often not obvious are depression and mild traumatic brain injury (MTBI). In my experience, depression is a common problem in evaluating an individual who complains of memory loss. The term "pseudo-dementia" is sometimes used to describe people, generally older adults, who complain of memory loss and who may perform poorly on memory tests, often because of inattention. Their cognitive problems are often the result of depression. Estimates of the prevalence of this condition vary widely, but it's probably in the range of ten percent of people who appear for memory evaluation. Discovery of pseudo-dementia is critical because depression can be successfully treated and the attendant memory problems completely resolved.

In practice, we administer the Affective Rating Scale (ARS) developed by Dr. Jerome Yesavage and his colleagues at Stanford University. If someone scores in the depressed or marginal range, we further investigate to determine if her memory problems are the result of depression. A copy of the ARS and instructions can be found in this book as Appendix 3.

MTBI is also a frequent cause of memory and attentional problems. If the frontal lobes are involved, there may also be problems
with organizational and reasoning skills. The most frequent causes
are automobile, motorcycle and bicycle accidents; falls; and blows to
the head during sports, assaults, or from accidents in the workplace.
Other traumas leading to a diagnosis of MTBI range from near
drowning to electrical shock. Criteria for a diagnosis of MTBI
include brief retrograde amnesia following a blow to the head or
other physical trauma (that is, inability to remember events just
prior to the incident), post-traumatic amnesia that can extend up to
twenty-four hours, and a transient alteration or loss of consciousness
that does not exceed thirty minutes.

Most cognitive problems resulting from MTBI are quickly
resolved, but deficits may persist six months or more. When memory problems suddenly develop, particularly in young people,
MTBI should be considered. Unfortunately, all too often this diagnosis is not considered because the trauma may be dismissed as not
serious enough to cause such problems.

So, in summary, many factors other than age can cause memory
problems. These problems can be often be treated, so sit down and
talk with your physician if you or a loved one are having a problem.
Persuade your doctor that consideration of the problem is worth
more than two or three minutes of her time. Go over the possibilities I list here and make sure that something other than "normal"
aging is not responsible. Everyone suffering memory loss deserves
that consideration.

4

Techniques for Improving Your Memory

I don't know how many books have been written on techniques for improving memory but, as of this writing, a search on Amazon.com lists 510 books and audio programs on "memory improvement,"—two of which I wrote myself. This number pales next to the 2,279 listings for "weight loss," but it is nevertheless quite impressive. While the ultimate message of all diet books is "eat less" or "exercise more," different authors provide colorful, and innovative means to achieve these two goals. By contrast, the overlap in advice is striking among memory improvement books, including my previous books on the subject. Pick up almost any of these books and you will learn about "chunking" numbers, using rhymes, forming acronyms and so on. There is remarkably little variation from book to book, and anyone who wants to learn these sometimes quite useful techniques has at least 510 books and a seemingly endless supply of magazine articles at his disposal. So, let's look at ways to improve memory from a somewhat different perspective.

The Value of Forgetting

Memories are not like money; the more you have, the better off you are. It is highly maladaptive in any animal or insect species—including man in the first category and most ex-husbands in the latter—to store in the brain every bit of information that strikes the sensory organs. There are filters deep in the mammalian brain, such as the ascending reticular activating system (RAS) near the base of the brain, that selectively control information that reaches the hippocampus and cerebral cortex and, indeed, information that reaches awareness. There are also direct neural connections between sensory organs and specialized brain regions—the eyes and the visual cortex at the back of the skull, for example. Here, too, perceptual processes screen out the vast majority of stimuli that reach the sense organs. Much of this sensory data is "judged" of insufficient importance to the organism to enter memory or even conscious awareness. Of the information that passes through these filters, the vast majority is still of insufficient importance to the organism to be saved for future reference, and it is important that such information never go beyond a memory buffer or, if it does, that it be forgotten.

Of course, just as it is important that irrelevant information be screened from memory, so too is it critical that information of vital interest to the survival of the organism not be screened out and that it receive high priority to enter the hippocampus and cerebral cortex. As discussed previously, this is where the amygdala and other brain regions come into play. So, forgetting is a natural part of this information screening process and is adaptive. That is, it is adaptive as long as it screens out information that is not useful in the future. However, as you know, when it screens out information that is useful, such as your neighbor's name, or even absolutely critical, such as the date of your wedding anniversary, memory loss can be highly problematic, indeed.

Step One in improving your memory follows directly from this discussion, that is: ***Do not try to remember everything unless you want to make a career of Trivial Pursuit.*** Know your limitations and concentrate on what will be important in the future. There is nothing adaptive about remembering the name of a taxi driver (who's no doubt a fine fellow, but who you are highly unlikely to ever meet again). At a business meeting, focus on remembering the names of only a few people with whom you are most likely to inter- act with in the future. Start with only their first name; you can add on their last name later, and do all those things you can learn in all those other memory books. Repeat the name, make it meaningful and associate a visual image of the name with a distinct facial fea- ture, and so on. This may seem obvious, but as you consciously practice this step, you will see how much of what you try to remem- ber is of little importance in your life, or how it may be of impor- tance for only a very limited period of time.

Step Two also derives from this adaptive process of filtering infor- mation that enters memory, or even consciousness, and, that is, *Pay attention. Focus like a laser beam on that relatively small amount of information that will be important to you in the future.* Ninety percent of the problem in "forgetting" names is that they were never learned in the first place. Instead of hearing a name at the time of introduction, repeating it, and making it meaning- ful, most of us are focusing on what we are going to say next, won- dering what the other person thinks of us, surveying others in the crowd and so on. Once again, most of the people you meet, unless you are attending a gathering for the closest friends of Mother Teresa, will not be worth remembering. Most of what you read should be forgotten. Every single bit of information preceded by the phrases "as they say" or "there is no doubt that" should immediate- ly be erased before it can enter memory and contaminate the frontal lobes, where judgments are made.

Step Three is more complicated than the first two steps and is related to mood and motivation, as well as to memory. In this case, we must consider the value of forgetting a powerful, vivid memory that was formed earlier because it was then important for the sur- vival of the individual, but that has since become maladaptive or even a threat to the individual's survival. Such memories may be of childhood trauma, wartime horror, psychological abandonment or personal failure.

These memories are no longer adaptive because the context in which they arose has changed and yet they persist and may result in pain, self-doubt, fear, dysphoria and failure in important tasks of daily life. We all have these memories, although they are of varying importance in our lives. They range from the Little League strike-out with the bases loaded in the ninth inning, to the horror of death and mutilation on the battlefield. The events that one remembers may well seem trivial to others, but they may have been magnified so greatly in memory that they lie at the center of one's self image. It's here that the value of forgetting is most profound.

Step Three is as follows: ***Challenge the importance of negative memories.*** Whether they are accurate is not the question. In fact, it is beside the point. What is to be challenged is whether these memories are useful. If your memory of paternal rejection for a poor report card in the fourth grade helps motivate you to excel and causes no great pain, by all means use it to good purpose, but if it lowers your self-worth and inhibits you in dealing with others, consider the "value of forgetting." Here is how to forget:

- Play out the negative memory in your mind as vividly as possible.
- Ask, "What does this memory mean about me at the time the experience occurred?"
- Ask "How has my situation changed since then?"
- Ask, "How am I different now than I was then?"
- Play the memory out again and pay attention to the feelings that arise as the memory begins to unfold. Learn to identify the feelings associated with the memory.
- Ask, "How is this memory helping or harming my life?"
- Ask, "Do I want to block this memory from my consciousness?"
- If the answer is "Yes," think of your greatest triumph in life.

- Rehearse this memory in detail. ("Who was present? What were you wearing? How did you feel?") Create a mental DVD of the good memory.
- When the first sign of the feelings associated with the mal-adaptive memory or the memory itself recurs, and often this will be at night and during light sleep, "eject it from your mind as if it were a DVD" and "insert" the positive memory track in your mind, play it several times. You will feel a sense of relaxation.
- As you use this technique, the memory will occur less and less frequently and will eventually fade from your mind. Such is the therapeutic power of forgetting.

Over the years, I have seen many patients who remembered events from their past, sometimes whole periods of their life, "too well." One such patient was a thirty-eight-year-old engineer, Terry, who worked for a large aerospace company and was referred to me because of complaints of depression and difficulty sleeping. In our first session, I learned that Terry was married and had two pre-adolescent sons. He reported that his wife was a successful attorney and that his family life was happy and fulfilling. Terry indicated, though, that his wife was worried that he had changed in the last two or three years, that he no longer seemed enthusiastic about life, and that he seemed perpetually tired and had great difficulty remaining asleep at night. A complete physical examination had revealed nothing likely to account for these symptoms. Terry acknowledged that his wife's observations were probably accurate, and indicated that he thought the problems were the result of his unhappiness with his job. He indicated that he loved the technical aspects of the job, but that he had been "passed over" for higher paying and more prestigious management jobs on several occasions, even though the individual select-ed had less relevant engineering experience. In the most recent case, the individual selected also had no advanced degree whereas Terry had a Master of Business Administration degree gained through several years of evening and weekend coursework. The explanation given by higher management the first time Terry was passed over was that the individual chosen had served in the Air Force and had more "leadership experience." On the second occasion, the individual chosen had no military experience, yet was said to have greater "leadership potential." On the most recent occasion, Terry didn't even bother to ask why he wasn't chosen.

In subsequent weeks, it became clear that Terry did indeed lack leadership skills. He simply had no experience. As a child, he wore thick eyeglasses and played no team sports. In neighborhood pick-up games of baseball or basketball, he was picked only when no one else was available and he clearly remembered the embarrassment of not being picked at all. One particularly clear memory was of a Spring, after-school, pick-up baseball game when Terry was four-teen years old. He was not picked to play, but was assigned as first base umpire. A few boys and a large group of girls were gathered in the stands to watch and Terry was quite proud of his role as an "offi-cial." On one play, late in the game, he dutifully called a much larg-er player "out" at first base. Rather than accept the call, the larger boy screamed at him "you four-eyed ..." and proceeded to attack. He quickly overcame Terry with multiple blows to the head and body. The bully knocked off Terry's glasses, crushed them under-foot, and then delivered a bone-shattering kick to the face. The attack was only halted when a horrified group of girls intervened. After that, Terry withdrew altogether from sports and virtually all male-dominated group activities. Through high school and college, he maintained contact only with a few close friends who he acknowledged were "science nerds."

The memory of his humiliation on the ball field had been rerun through Terry's mind so many thousands of times and was so deeply ingrained that he could describe the taste of the dirt he swallowed and the unfocused, hazy look of pity on the face of one of the girls who came to his aid. Clearly, this was a memory best forgotten.

I employed the techniques outlined to rid Terry of the memory. We found that his proudest moment came when he won a regional science fair in high school and, with the help a retrieved photo of Terry accepting the prize, with his beaming parents and grandparents looking on, we set about creating a "replacement memory" for that which was so maladaptive. We also spoke of how Terry was a rightful leader and "star" of an engineering team and used an excellent set of tapes on leadership skills to help teach specific techniques. As it turned out, Terry was not promoted at his company, but left after several months to take a managerial job at a competing company across the country. For the next three or four years, I received Christmas cards from Terry telling me how happy he and his family were and how well things were going at work, but then I suspect it became adaptive for the memory of psychotherapy to be moved from the forefront of consciousness and largely "forgotten" too.

The Power of Association

As we discussed, the brain and our perceptual systems filter out information that is not adaptive. Of course, what is adaptive will differ from person-to-person and from time-to-time in the same person. I, for example, drove the same car for fifteen years and paid almost no attention to other cars on the road. I was completely unable to distinguish a Honda from a Toyota or a Ford from a Chevrolet (except for the Mustang which still looks as I recall it did four decades ago). Then, recently, I was faced with the choice between very expensive repairs or a new car, and I began to notice every detail of every interesting car on the road. In the end, I saw no car I liked better than my own and I opted for the repairs. So, once again I've become oblivious to the brands of vehicles on the road, but for a period of a month or so, my criteria for adaptive information had changed. Information entered my secondary memory that would have been filtered out before. And now again it's filtered out after I've finished entertaining the frivolous notion of replacing a car before it is even twenty years old.

To prevent information from being filtered out in short term memory, and this assumes you have paid attention and even let the information into short term memory, you must trick your brain into accepting that the new information is adaptive for your well being —or, in other words, it will be useful to you.

One way to do that is to associate the new information with other information that has already passed the adaptivity test and is stored in the brain. Thus, the telephone number "413-555-1647" can be held in working memory by a healthy young person (usually with difficulty), as long as it is continuously rehearsed and there is no interruption before the number is dialed. However, except for extraordinary individuals, it must be converted into something meaningful if it is to enter long-term memory. So use what you have in long-term memory to make it meaningful, or at least reduce the meaningless information to be remembered. For instance, for me, my old area code was "410," so I take the first two digits from that, my son's age is 35 and, so now I have 413 5, and the last digit is repeated twice, so I have 413 555. For 16, I think "sweet sixteen" and the 47 from a 747 airliner so I now have the phone number 413-555-1647. We will speak of visualization in the next section of the book, but I can use this associative information to form an image of my son making a phone call from our old home to his daughter when she is sixteen and planning to fly off on vacation aboard a 747.

The point is, associate what is to be remembered with what is already in long term memory. In the case of numbers, use ages of friends and family members, birthdays, historical dates, times of day, road numbers, addresses, phone numbers, numbers of sports figures, or hundreds of thousand of other numbers you have already stored in memory. Try to take several numbers that you dial frequently but have not memorized and convert them in this manner. It really becomes quite easy with time.

In the case of names, if it's possible, associate the name you want to remember with names of people you already know. Of course, once again, this assumes you were paying attention and "got" the name in the first place. For example, before my son was married, my wife and I met the parents of his lovely wife-to-be and had a very pleasant conversation. Several years later, while driving up the California coast to the wedding, I turned to my wife and asked "What is the name of Cyndi's dad?" She looked at me as if I were hopelessly slow and said, "Tom." So, I guess I just wasn't listening because that is also my name and would not require too abstract an association. Another association technique that I find very helpful is to look at the person and pick a distinguishing feature—say, the eyes. Then convert the name to a visual image and place the image over the eyes. In the case of "Tom," the image may be of "tom-tom" drums, or the helmets previously worn by British "tommys," or a "tom cat" or "tom turkey" or "tommy gun" and so on. Or, let's take Dan who has long hair. I, in that case, could form an image of Dan wearing a coon skin hat, like Daniel Boone. Of course that' is a little tricky because that image is also consistent with Davy Crocket and "Dave."

You also do not necessarily have to have a specific facial feature. You can form an image of Tony's face on a Tony Award, or Frank in a frankfurter roll, or Doug might be imagined wearing Douglas MacArthur's hat and smoking his corncob pipe, or Mike speaking into a microphone, and on and on. For last names, once again associate the new name with names already stored in your memory or made up from your own verbal associations or visual images. You might also consult Appendix 6 for symbols you might associate with the 150 most common family names in the United States. Of course, these association techniques will work somewhat less well if you are traveling in Kurdistan.

Two or three years ago, I was reminded of the power of association techniques when I visited the Sonesta Beach Hotel on Key Biscayne, just across the causeway from Miami. I had visited the hotel many times for an annual professional meeting, but had not been back since 1985—that is, for nearly twenty years. The hotel looked entirely different from what I remembered, much smaller and less grand. Of course I recognized no one inside the hotel. When I walked out to the pool though, the bartender turned to me and said "By hook or by crook, Dr. Crook, how are you?" His name was Gino, which I recalled immediately upon seeing his nametag. This, by any standard, was a remarkable demonstration of Gino's cognitive abilities and also the power of association. The hotel has approximately 600 rooms and the average stay is certainly no longer that two or three days, so each of the rooms occupy at least 100 people per year (usually with their spouses), so that is 60,000 visitors per year for 18 years or well over a million people. Remarkable, but I couldn't bring myself to ask Gino whether his association was purely verbal or into which of my facial features the hooks were imbedded. It was an image I would rather not live with.

Visualize

As noted in the first chapter, the occipital lobe at back of the brain is the primary area for processing and storage of visual information and is often called the visual cortex. In addition to this area, there are at least thirty areas of the human cortex that process and store visual information. Far more of the human cortex is devoted to visual input than to information supplied by other sensory modalities. In the African elephant, by comparison, brain areas devoted to visual processing and storage are quite small relative to areas associated with olfaction. The elephant captures air in his trunk and then blows it into his mouth near the bottom of the lower lip where powerful olfactory receptors are located. The smell is compared with millions of others stored in the elephant's cortex and on the basis of that comparison the animal remains calm, flees, charges an enemy, or locates food and water. He will also remember for his lifetime the specific smell associated with every river he crosses, every tree he rubs, and every threat he encounters. I have lived in Southeast

Africa and always marveled at how well the sense organs and brain morphology have evolved to meet the needs of all species.

Because so much of our brain circuitry is devoted to vision, it can prove helpful to convert what we wish to remember into visual images. We have already considered the use of visual associations in remembering names, but let's consider other ways that visualization can be helpful. Let's begin with a story told by the Roman orator Cicero about an event said to have occurred around the year 500 B.C. The story is that Scopas, a Greek nobleman, hired Simonides, a well-known lyrical poet, to perform for himself and his guests to celebrate a wrestling victory. Simonides' poem was to praise Scopas, but Simonides also included a passage praising the twin gods Castor and Pollux. Angry at their inclusion, Scopas threatened to pay Simonides only half the amount agreed upon and told him sarcastically that he could collect the rest from Castor and Pollux. As the matter was being discussed, Simonides was told that two young men were asking to see him just outside the door. He went outside and saw no one, and just as he was about to return, the roof of the building collapsed, crushing Scopas and his guests under tons of stone. Castor and Pollux had avenged the lack of respect shown by Scopos, and had rewarded Simonides by sparing his life. As the rubble was cleared in subsequent days, it was found that the bodies were crushed beyond recognition and grieving family members sought to identify the remains of their loved ones. Simonides came to their aid, recalling where each guest was seated as he moved from seat to seat in his memory and, thus, was born the method of loci (places).

Simonides then reasoned that the same technique would work with the long poems that he memorized and recited. He imagined moving around a table in which sections of the poem were piled in each chair. Rather than memorize the entire poem, he could mentally move from chair to chair picking up and reading the papers staked in each. Cicero and other subsequent orators used the method of loci in delivering hours-long lectures. They would, for example, create memory palaces with many rooms and place in each room those thoughts that would let them recall all their points by walking through the memory palace.

Today we speak from notes and teleprompters and hardly need to construct "memory palaces." Nevertheless, the ancient technique can be useful. If you have a series of tasks to perform, imagine yourself performing a task in a room of your house and simply walk through your house as the day progresses. Or, if you are a golfer, use the 18 holes and 18 greens to place information to be remembered. The method of loci lends itself to tasks ranging from public speaking to grocery shopping and includes: remembering the sequential tasks to be performed in a day or week, the people one must contact, the order of thoughts that one wishes to express in a conversation, the tasks one must complete in order to reach a goal, and so on. On an interpersonal level, one can place each of his loved ones in rooms or boxes with the thought he wishes to express each day, and walk through those boxes each evening to be sure a twelve-year-old daughter is told she is beautiful, a wife is told how lucky her husband is to be with her, a husband is told what a good man he is, and all those kind and supportive words are not forgotten. This is the essence of a good memory: it is not whether one remembers to buy toothpaste when shopping.

As a boy in Baltimore, I witnessed the method of loci in action, even though I had no idea what it was. My barber, Mr. John, a close friend of my father was also the local "bookie." He was a good-hearted fellow who believed in saving his customers, including many longshoreman and shipyard workers, the trouble of driving to Maryland race tracks, such as Pimlico, to bet on races. In the spirit of a good citizenship, Mr. John would simply allow his customers to bet with him at the same odds offered by the race tracks. He spoke on the phone almost continuously through the day, with the phone tucked between his shoulder and cheek as he cut hair. He took hundreds of bets everyday and never wrote anything down. Such betting was, of course, illegal, but written evidence was generally required for a conviction. Mr. John could not only remember every bet every day and the outcome of every race, but he would settle books with his clients at each haircut, sometimes after they had won or lost on dozens of races.

You can imagine the temptation of someone who had made quite a large wager and lost, to deny that he had ever made such a bet. I never saw or heard of such a claim and never knew if that was because of community respect for Mr. John's memory abilities or his Sicilian heritage but, in any case, there was never a dispute. Thanks to Mr. John, I was employed as a longshoreman on the docks in Baltimore and that helped me work my way through college. When I returned to the neighborhood years later I asked how he could remember all that information. Mr. John (I never dropped the "Mr.") gave me an explanation that could have come from Simonides. He said he could visualize an extended "racing sheet" in which every customer had a row with multiple columns extending to the right. He visualized the results of every race in a box and could mentally carry forward to the far right column where he calculated the amount owed or due at each haircut. Through such visualization techniques, Mr. John conducted this important community service work for decades.

It's is helpful to reinforce any verbal information one wishes to remember with a visual image. So, in remembering first and last names, "Bob Smith" can be converted to an image (depending on one's age) of Bob Hope as a blacksmith, or "Sponge Bob" bending under the weight of the blacksmith's hammer. Joe Shaoul, a friend of mine, can be remembered by an image of Joe Lewis with a towel (rhymes with Shaoul) hanging from his neck; Kay Grant, my wife's maiden name, can be pictured wearing a Union General's hat with a large "K" on the front; Charles Nelson, another friend, can be seen as Prince Charles locked in a full nelson wrestling hold, and on and on. These verbal associations combined with a visual image are particularly resistant to forgetting.

Create a Prosthetic Memory Environment

I could have carried the visualization discussion into all sorts of other applications, as many other authors of memory books do, but, frankly, it seems easier to me to make a grocery list than to construct fanciful images such as a chicken and cow drinking coffee while sugar is falling from the sky in order to help you remember to buy eggs, milk, coffee and sugar at the grocery store. Many such memory techniques seem to me just plain silly when it is quite simple to keep a grocery list on the kitchen counter, to which items are added when it becomes apparent they are needed.

About twenty-five years ago I had the opportunity to meet and briefly work with B. F. Skinner, arguably the most influential psychologist of the Twentieth century. Many of you will recall from your college days the films of pigeons playing ping-pong (with their beaks) and animals doing all sorts of unlikely things because they had been trained through operant conditioning—simply rewarding desired behaviors in very precise ways—to perform behaviors that would not be performed in nature. Dr. Skinner and his many followers—known as "behaviorists" or behavioral psychologists—later used these same techniques with schoolchildren, prisoners, mental patients and many others in a process that came to be known as "behavior modification." When I met Dr. Skinner, he was in his late seventies and still at his desk at Harvard. He had become interested in aging and memory, and he frequently discussed the concept of a prosthetic environment for the brain, just as prosthetic environments are created for those with physical disabilities. With regard to memory, he was very fond of the notion that, as one ages, one should "rely on memo's not memories." Professor Skinner remained an advocate of rigorous mental exercise, but he would have scoffed at the idea of performing difficult memory tricks instead of simply keeping a list.

Among the principal elements of the prosthetic environment, the first is organization—essentially, "A place for everything and everything in its place." This alone will reduce the vast majority of problems most of us face in misplacing objects. Notes and written schedules also play an important part, as can sticky notes and refrigerator magnets. Notes are helpful well beyond the grocery store. They are helpful when making a telephone call, for example, lest one hang up without making an important point. A table or container near the door can also be important if the thought "I must drop off my clothes at the cleaner tomorrow" is followed by gathering up the clothes and placing them near the door one must exit en route to work. Various other devices, such as timers and pill containers that alert an individual when medications should be taken can be very helpful. These also contribute to the prosthetic environment for memory, as do multiple pairs of inexpensive eyeglasses placed in different rooms around the house and multiple house keys placed in strategic locations.

Those readers with family members in their late seventies, eighties and nineties might particularly want to examine their relative's environment at home. Many of these people were profoundly affected by the Great Depression of the 1930s and are inclined to save almost everything of conceivable value. Later in life, when memory capacities are diminished, this tendency can present problems, as the telephone and heating bills are stacked with everything else that came in the mail. You may be able to help them greatly in their day-to-day life by reducing clutter and helping to build an environment where they are less likely to have dangerous or costly memory failures.

All-in-All

The lessons of this chapter are that one should be quite selective in what one chooses to remember. Do as your brain and perceptual organs do: only remember what is likely to be useful in the future. Some of what you now remember is probably best forgotten, and we have discussed techniques for blocking memories that are not adaptive. Sometimes, though, you must fool your brain into recognizing that something abstract—such as a name or number—will be adaptive in the future, and that it should be stored in your long-term memory. As we discussed, one of the most effective ways to do this is through association techniques, whereby the new information is paired with information already in memory. Another effective technique is to visualize what is to be remembered rather than store the information solely as a verbal memory. Finally, we discussed the importance of organization and of creating a prosthetic environment for memory. Together, you will find these techniques quite helpful.

5

Drugs and Dietary Supplements to Improve Memory

Attempts to treat memory loss with drugs and dietary supplements can be traced back over many centuries. Indeed, galantamine, one of the five drugs approved in the United States to treat Alzheimer's disease, is actually a derivative of the snow drop plant that may have been used more than 3,000 years ago by the ancient Greeks. The well-known gingko biloba extract, sold as a dietary supplement to improve memory, is derived from an eponymous tree that is probably the oldest surviving species on earth, perhaps 200 million years old. Use of leaves and bark from the tree to treat the brain is described in a Chinese medical text dating to 2800 B.C., nearly 5,000 years ago. Despite this long history, there is no drug approved in the United States today to treat memory loss in people who are not suffering from dementia. The five drugs that are approved for treating Alzheimer's dementia are all modestly and temporarily effective. They all have multiple side-effects and are generally not appropriate for treating non-demented people.

Products to Preserve Memory from the Effects of Aging, Stress, Brain Insult and Disease

There are two basic categories of dietary supplements, also called "nutraceutical" products, sold for memory improvement. The first is composed of products that are really not intended to improve memory in days, weeks, or months, but are intended to nourish the brain and protect it from damage as we grow older and face stresses and insults that contribute to brain aging. These products include omega-3 free fatty acids (FFAs). There is a growing body of sound evidence that omega-3 supplementation is important for the developing brains of fetuses and children and also the brains, as well as hearts, of mature adults. There are three omega-3 FFAs and these are ALA (alpha linoleic acid), EPA (eicosapentaenoic acid), and DHA (docosahexaenoic acid). ALA can be converted to EPA and DHA, although the process is inefficient, and it is derived from flaxseed, nuts and various oils. EPA and DHA are most commonly derived from oily fish such as tuna, salmon and mackerel, although DHA can be derived from marine algae. Because it is free of contaminants that may be found in fish, this form is now used in most infant formulas. Although DHA is the primary structural component of brain tissue, and DHA supplementation alone is probably adequate for the fetus, infant, and toddler, the mature adult brain probably benefits from EPA supplementation as well. I believe that daily supplementation with a fish oil product is beneficial, but care must be exercised in selecting a product that is not likely to be contaminated with mercury or other metals. Such contaminants are most likely to be found in farmed salmon or other fish rather than free ranging cold water fish. An excellent omega-3 source is Natural Factors® Wild Alaskan Salmon Oil (1000 mg).

In addition to an omega-3 product, it is probably worthwhile to make sure that your multivitamin contains an adequate amount of Vitamin E. That powerful antioxidant can inhibit the destructive effects of oxidation in the brain and elsewhere in the body. If your daily vitamin does not contain at least 250 IU (international units), you may want to switch to another product or add a separate vitamin E capsule to your daily regimen. I take (and recommend) 400 IU of a natural form of Vitamin E, that is "d" alpha (α) tocopherol—not "dl" alpha tocopherol, which is the much less active synthetic form.

Beyond these dietary supplements, and with one exception, I would be wary of the many, many products that are said to protect the brain from aging and insult. The exception is another old, inexpensive and wonderfully effective product: aspirin. A major threat to the aging brain is stroke and related vascular events. Vitamin E at the doses I recommended has anti-coagulant effects, but an 81 mg. baby aspirin taken once daily (if it does not cause gastrointestinal irritation) has well-established anti-coagulant effects and positive effects on blood platelet aggregation. This will be beneficial in preventing vascular accidents for adults over, perhaps, fifty and, certainly, sixty years of age and older.

Products to Improve Memory

Drugs

Rather than being designed simply to protect the brain and limit further memory loss, there are also both supplements and drugs designed to *improve* memory in hours, days, weeks, or months. No such drugs are approved by the Food and Drug Administration (FDA) in the United States for AAMI. However, drugs that are approved in the United States for medical conditions other than memory loss are sometimes taken for that purpose "off-label." By the way, don't believe the stories you may read about the remarkable drugs for memory that are available overseas but blocked from sale in the U.S. by the FDA. There are no such drugs. The drugs approved for memory loss in European countries are mainly the so-called "nootropic" (toward the mind) drugs of which piracetam is the prototype. There are many published studies with these drugs and my colleagues and I studied a number of them for the treatment of AAMI in the late 1980s and the1990s. Despite substantial sales in Europe, then and now, we were unable to confirm any benefit of these compounds in healthy older subjects with age-related memory loss. That is also true of, literally, dozens of drugs designed by the leading multi-national pharmaceutical companies to treat AAMI or related disorders. This is true, even though most of these drugs were designed on a sound theoretical basis and did improve learning and memory in aged animals.

Among drugs approved in the United States for medical or psychiatric conditions that may be prescribed by physicians "off-label" to improve memory are the stimulants, amphetamines and methylphenidate (Ritalin), approved to treat attention deficit hyperactivity disorder (ADHD) and modafanil (Pro-Vigil), which is approved for excessive daytime sleepiness and narcolepsy. These drugs have the capacity to maintain cognitive performance and temporarily offset the effects of fatigue. There are likely arenas, such as the battlefield, where they can be useful, but I know of no evidence that they are useful in improving memory abilities diminished by age, stress, neurological disease, or the many other factors previously discussed that can cause memory loss. Stimulants also have physiological and psychological side effects that argue strongly against their use, except in conditions for which such use was approved by the FDA.

Older Dietary Supplements

In contrast to drugs, there are many dietary supplements, or nutraceuticals, that are sold with a claim that they improve memory, or more generally, mental performance. This is possible because the principal federal law governing the sale of such products—the Dietary Supplement Health and Education Act (DSHEA), passed in 1994—limits the power of the FDA over dietary supplement makers and allows producers to make "structure and function claims" (e.g., improves memory) on the basis of far less evidence than is required in the case of a drug. Indeed, no approval is needed to bring a product to market and evidence to support efficacy must be provided only if a supplement maker is challenged, usually by the Federal Trade Commission (FTC) rather than the FDA.

Often, as in the case of top-selling brands such as Focus Factor® and Senior Moment®, there is no evidence of efficacy of the product sold. Rather, the products are mixtures of various dietary supplements and usually any evidence of efficacy cited comes from studies of one or more of the components, not the mixture itself. Many, many drugs and dietary supplements interact with one another and, in these combination products, there is no consideration of such possible interactions. Usually, too, the dosage of each component product is far lower than the dosage tested in the studies that are cited. Most important, though, is that there is usually no scientifically sound evidence to support the evidence of each component of the product, even if it were administered in the dose said to be shown effective. Let us look at the most common substances sold alone or in combination and consider the evidence of efficacy in AAMI or comparable populations.

- *Ginkgo Biloba.* Sales of various ginkgo products (Ginkoba, GinkGold, etc., etc.) soared in the United States during the mid and late 1990s and may have reached total sales of $400 million dollars. Since then, a number of studies have been published that did not find ginkgo products effective in AAMI or similar populations and news stories have suggested that the products increase the risk of stroke. Partly as a result, sales have declined dramatically. Ginkgo extracts appear to affect blood flow in the brain, but the preponderance of evidence suggests they are not useful in treating AAMI or related conditions. These conditions do not appear related to decreased blood flow in the brain and neither drugs nor supplements such as ginkgo would be expected to be beneficial. The usual dose of the standard extract (Egb 761) is 120 to 240 mg. per day divided into two or three doses. Combination products may contain much less.

- *Acetyl L-Carnitine (ALC)* is derived from carnitine, a naturally occurring substance in the human body. It has been sold as a drug for many years in Europe and, for the past twelve years, as a dietary supplement in the United States. ALC helps the body metabolize fatty acids for energy and is important for energy utilization in every cell in the body. ALC has been studied for the treatment of a very wide variety of conditions including weight loss and heart disease, as well as Alzheimer's disease. Results in AD are, at best, equivocal and there is no sound evidence that ALC is effective in AAMI or related disorders. Nevertheless, it is sold as a dietary supplement for improving memory. The normal dose of ALC for a wide range of conditions is 500 to 2000 mg. per day, with higher doses divided into two or three times per day administration. Once again, combination products often contain often much less active compound.

- *Vinpocetine.* Once again, vinpocetine is a dietary supplement in the United States and a drug in almost fifty other countries. It was synthesized from the blue periwinkle plant in about 1960 and is used to treat a variety of conditions including cerebral vascular ischemia. It may have value in stroke and other vascular disorders that can impair memory and other cognitive functions, but there is no sound evidence that it is effective in AAMI or related disorders. Therapeutic doses of vinpocetine range from 20 to 60 mg. per day and it is expensive, so much lower doses will be found in many combination products.

- *Huperzine A (HPA).* Huperzine is an ancient Chinese herbal medicine that is prepared from the Chinese club moss and used to treat many disorders. HPA is an alkaloid that has the same properties of four drugs approved by the FDA in the United States to treat AD. That is, it is a so-called cholinesterase inhibitor that limits the breakdown of the neurotransmitter acetylcholine and, therefore, raises available acetylcholine levels in the brain. This neurotransmitter is critical for memory and decreased levels are characteristic of AD and AAMI. Unfortunately, there are no well- controlled studies supporting efficacy in AAMI or related disorders but, in theory, the compound could be modestly effective. Again, take care to avoid levels in combination products that are below the 50 mcg to 200 mcg. (micrograms, not milligrams) daily dose said to be effective.

- *Galantamine.* This is the ancient drug derived from the snow drop plant that I referred to earlier. It dates back to the ancient Greeks. Galantamine, like huperzine, is a cholinesterase inhibitor that raises levels of acetylcholine in the brain. In fact, it is one of the four such drugs approved in the United States to treat AD and yet, despite challenges from the FDA, it is also sold as a dietary supplement (because of a grandfather clause in the DSHEA legislation). Again, like huperzine, it may offer modest help in AAMI, but there are no studies demonstrating such an effect. Therapeutic doses of galantamine, when prescribed for AD, are usually 16 or 24 mg. daily.

- *Lecithin.* Lecithin is a primary source of phosphatidylcholine (PC), which is the precursor, or parent compound, from which acetylcholine is derived in the body. Lecithin, and before that choline chloride, were widely studied in the late 1970s and early 1980s as a treatment for AD. My colleagues and I later studied lecithin as a treatment for AAMI and, whereas some of the compounds we just discussed could have some modest therapeutic effects if they were studied carefully, lecithin has been studied carefully and I am convinced it has no such effects. Advocates of lecithin maintain that therapeutic doses are between 3 and 9 g. grams, not milligrams) daily in divided doses.

- *Phosphatidylserine (PS).* PS is a phospholipid like PC, and a critical part of the cell membrane in every cell of every living organism. As cells in the brain (and elsewhere else in the body) age, they can become rigid as cholesterol replaces the normal phospholipids. PS administration is thought to improve brain cell fluidity and improve transmission across the cell wall. PS also increases the availability of acetylcholine and affects other neurotransmitter systems that may be implicated in AAMI. It is particularly concentrated in brain cell membranes in mammals and, in fact, the PS compound my colleagues and I first studied in AAMI was derived from the brains of cattle slaughtered for human consumption. PS was first chemically isolated from the brains of cattle in 1948 and was approved as a drug in Italy and other European countries for treating what we now call AD and other generally ill-defined brain disorders. My colleagues at Stanford and Vanderbilt Universities and I conducted a very carefully controlled study in AAMI in 1989 through 1990 and reported our findings in the journal *Neurology* in 1991. We found statistically significant differences on a battery of neuropsychological tests when subjects administered 300 mg. PS daily for 12 weeks were compared with those given placebo for the same period. We did not find improvement in self-reported memory abilities, however. Subjects treated with PS performed better on memory tests, but did not perceive the improved performance. Soon after our paper was published, all PS research in humans abruptly ended because it was discovered in England, and later Europe, that humans who consumed tissue (particularly brain) from cattle with Bovine Spongiform Encephalopathy, mad cow disease, could develop a variant of a normally very rare and fatal dementing disorder known as Creutsfeld-Jakob Disease. It was not until the mid-1990s that PS products developed from vegetable sources came to the U.S. market and, whereas we had studied PS as a drug, the DSHEA legislation had been passed and it could be sold as a dietary supplement for memory loss. We conducted a study of one of these products, in which PS was derived from soybeans and reported, in 1998, results comparable to those seen with the bovine cortex-derived formulation. I continue to believe that PS can be a valuable supplement in AAMI, but several caveats are necessary. First, many of the vegetable derived PS products sold today have not been clinically tested. Second, we did not find that PS improved people's assessment of their own memory abilities. In other words, they did not think their memory had improved. This could obviously be a problem, in that people may not continue to take a product if they do not feel improvement. It may be, however, that people taking PS do recognize improvement after an extended period of administration. Our studies lasted only 12 weeks. And third, and probably most important, the dosage we found effective was 300 mg. per day. PS is expensive and the vast majority of PS or combination products on the market contain far less than the 300 mg. daily dose.

Twenty First Century Supplement Development for AAMI and Related Conditions

As I write, in the summer of 2006, I am surprised that dietary supplement companies continue to introduce products that are said to be new and exciting when they are, in fact, simply rehashed mixtures of the same old, often centuries-old, compounds. Take a look at products in your health food store or on the web and you will see the same products discussed above reappearing, usually at doses that would be ineffective even if the product worked.

Often, all sorts of B complex and other vitamins are added to the formula, even though there is no evidence that such vitamins improve memory in persons who are not vitamin deficient. Such conditions are very rare among persons in the U.S. considering a supplement for memory because, even in the face of deficient diets, nearly everyone seeking a supplement for memory is already taking an all-purpose vitamin and mineral supplement. In fact, adding multiple vitamins to memory supplements is much more likely to do harm than good.

A new product that I discovered soon after it was developed in 2003 is a neuropeptide compound identified as N-PEP-12. I was familiar with the parent drug of this compound: a mixture of 85% amino acids and 15% neuropeptides of low molecular weight. Neuropeptides are short chains of amino acids, the twenty molecules that form proteins under direction of genetic coding. NPs play diverse roles in the brain. They can influence cellular activity at the DNA level by altering gene structure to increase or decrease gene expression. Several neuropeptides, notably vasopressin (which is under the control of acetylcholine) and ACTH (adrenocorticotropic hormone), have been shown to play a role in learning and memory in animal studies and a few human trials. However, they are quite difficult to deliver exogenously to the brain and the magnitude of their effects in clinical trials has been small.

The parent drug of N-PEP-12, Cerebrolysin (CL), is sold in thirty-five countries for the treatment of a variety of brain insults and diseases, including AD. A severe limitation on CL use, though, that would preclude its use in AAMI, is that it must be delivered through intravenous infusion. Standard CL treatment consists of an infusion of 30 ml. CL mixed with 100 ml. saline for twenty minutes. This treatment is repeated fives day per week for four weeks, followed by an eight-week period off treatment, followed by a repetition of the four-week treatment period. This treatment regimen has been shown in large, multi-center trials to have significant benefits for as many as three months following treatment in AD and other neurological disorders. CL has been studied by leading teams of neuroscience researchers around the world and shown to have diverse effects that are associated with both acute improvement in learning and memory and in neuroprotection.

In terms of acute improvement in memory, glucose is the most important source of energy in the brain and available glucose is diminished in AAMI, and further diminished in AD and other brain disorders. Oral or intravenous administration of glucose can improve cognitive performance but very high doses must be administered, driving blood glucose dangerously high and, thus, this is not a practical treatment for memory disorders. CL, though, can raise glucose levels in the brain by facilitating glucose transport across the blood brain barrier (BBB). This is accomplished because CL up-regulates, or increases the expression, of a gene (GLUT-1) that partially controls the passage of glucose across the BBB. Because of this effect on glucose availability, CL has an immediate and pronounced effect on aerobic neuronal metabolism. This, in turn, may lead to improved learning and memory.

In addition to the effects of CL on glucose transport, effects of the compound relate to a remarkable and fascinating story that began developing in the later years of the twentieth century. This is the story of brain plasticity (or neural plasticity) that has, heretofore, had no influence on the development of dietary supplements for memory and is only beginning to influence the development of pharmaceutical products for neurological disorders such as AD.

It was believed only a few years ago that when a neuron died it could not regenerate. It was further believed that memories were formed largely through neurochemical events rather that the actual growth of new dendrites and even new neurons in critical areas of the brain such as the hippocampus. We now have excellent evidence that dendrites sprout to develop millions of new connections among neurons, that new neurons can grow and form millions of interconnections and that this growth may represent the formation of new memories. We know too that CL can facilitate these processes. Evidence published in international neuroscience journals demonstrates that CL enhances synaptic density and neuronal transmission in the hippocampus and entorhinal cortex (an area important for memory). It also, increases the density and expression of glutamate (an important neurotransmitter) receptors in the hippocampus and elsewhere in the brain, increases neuronal connectivity in critical brain areas and counters decreased neuronal plasticity in aged rats. In young rats, CL improves dendritic arborization (sprouting of branches, much like a tree in Spring), effects dendritic length and synaptic density, and improves neuronal plasticity by inducing neurite (immature neuron) growth and synapse formation. Many of the effects of CL mimic those of endogenous nerve growth factor (NGF) which, as one would expect, diminishes with advancing age. NGF is synthesized in the hippocampus and transported to neurons in the basal forebrain where it stimulates cholinergic activity and facilitates learning and memory. Exogenous NGF cannot be administered because it does not cross the BBB, but CL does cross and mimics NGF.

On the neuroprotective side, CL protects cholinergic neurons from the neurotoxic effects of chemicals (glutamate) and lesions (fimbria-fornex) that would normally destroy them. It has anti-apoptic effects (that is, it protects against programmed cell death), it promotes cholinergic fiber regeneration, and it reduces the beta amaloid plaque (a hallmark of AD) burden in the aged brain. CL also reduces microglial activation and exerts a neuro-immunotrophic activity that reduces the extent of inflammation and accelerated neuronal death that occurs under various pathologic conditions.

CL is produced by biotechnological methods, using a proteolytic breakdown of purified porcine brain proteins. It is produced by EBEWE Pharmaceuticals, a venerable Austrian pharmaceutical company that was once, through corporate acquisitions, a unit of Abbott Pharmaceuticals. All production is done to international pharmaceutical standards—not the far more relaxed standards of many dietary supplement companies. Recognizing the limitations of a compound that must be delivered through intravenous infusion, and recognizing that a less potent version of CL might suffice in AAMI rather than in AD and other dementing disorders, EBEWE turned it's research and product development technology to developing a faithful, but less potent version of CL, that could be orally administered. The product that emerged in 2003 was N-PEP-12 and my colleagues and I had the privilege of conducting the first clinical trial of that compound in AAMI.

We conducted a very careful, fully randomized, placebo-controlled trial among fifty-four healthy persons over the age of fifty with "normal" age-related memory loss (i.e., AAMI). The average age of study subjects was sixty eight years old, and the duration of the trial was thirty days, with standardized cognitive testing and both clinical and self evaluations conducted prior to dosing and, again, at the conclusion of treatment. The tests used include more difficult versions of the same tests used by pharmaceutical companies to obtain approval for the AD drugs on the market in the U.S.

The vast majority of the clinical trials I have conducted have been negative and, so, I never expect positive results, even when the idea behind the trial is sound. I was particularly cautious in this case because the treatment period was only one month. With the drugs currently approved in the U.S. for AD, for example, no differences between drug and placebo are seen until at least three and often six months of treatment.

Nevertheless, we did find highly statistically significant differences between drug- and placebo-treated subjects on memory test scores. This was the first time, in my experience, that a nutraceutical product for memory had succeeded in a clinical trial since my colleagues and I found PS effective in 1991. (We confirmed that finding in 1998.) With PS, though, we found improvement only on test scores and study subjects did not report that their memory had improved. With N-PEP-12 we found evidence of efficacy on self and clinical evaluations, as well as memory tests. We published our findings in the journal *International Psychopharmacology* in 2005 and, since then, we and other investigators have published electrophysiological and other evidence that the effects of N-PEP-12 are parallel to CL.

Beginning in 2005, N-PEP-12 was brought to the market in the U.S. as a dietary supplement under the brand name MemoProve®. I had the opportunity recently to interview a number of people now taking MemoProve and following is a representative interview.

Jane M. was a sixty-two-year-old woman who complained about memory loss affecting her performance in her job as a commercial real estate broker. She complained that she would confuse conversations she had with different real estate brokers, tenants, or landlords. She had confused, for example, a rate given to one prospective tenant with a rate given to another in an entirely different building. Jane's mother died in her mid-eighties, having suffered profound memory loss, probably due to Alzheimer's disease, in the last several years of her life. Thus, it was not too surprising that Jane began to worry that she was at an early stage of Alzheimer's disease. I explained to her the magnitude of "normal" memory loss that can occur by age sixty-two, suggested that she have a thorough medical evaluation and agreed to provide her with N-PEP-12 after the evaluation was completed. The interview that follows occurred three months after she began taking the compound.

T.C.: Would you be kind enough to describe the memory problems that led to the concern you had at the time you came in for an evaluation?

J.M.: Well, I had always had a really outstanding memory. I graduated in the top ten percent of my college class, and right out of college I took a job in the securities industry. At that time, there weren't many women in the industry, except in secretarial or low level administrative roles—at least that was true in the part of the industry where I worked in New York. I was very concerned that I had to be every bit as sharp as my male colleagues and probably sharper if I hoped to get ahead. In the first month or two, I was a nervous wreck and very concerned that I would make a costly mistake, but as time went on, I became very comfortable that I could do mental calculations and make decisions as quickly as anyone I worked with. My memory for numbers became really phenomenal and I could think on my feet as quickly as anyone. I worked in the industry for seven years and left only after I had been married for a year and a half and became pregnant with my first daughter. Over the next five years, I had two other children and became a "stay at home mom." I did not go back to work until my youngest daughter went off to college, although all the years I was home, I was actively involved in all sorts of activities related to the kids' school and many extracurricular activities. I also remained as I am now, an avid reader. I tried to keep up with technical advances and that was actually not too difficult since my husband and all three of my kids are sort of "computer geeks." In going back to the workplace, I first took a course to get my commercial real estate license. I surprised myself by doing very well in the course, even though I was well into my fifties and, although there were people of all ages, some of the students were fresh out of college. I began work with a firm that was very informal and I really enjoyed my work. However, it seemed to me they had too many agents for the amount of business conducted and I sometimes came home at the end of the day having accomplished nothing. So, after eighteen months, I joined the firm I work for now and, boy, was that different. From the start, it was a go-go atmosphere where the phone never stopped ringing and I was dealing with dozens and dozens of people everyday. I use to be amazed at how quickly the day passed. I really enjoyed the work and I actually began to make enough money that my husband was impressed. Even though the job was pretty stressful and very fast paced, it was not nearly as difficult as my job trading securities. Still, I was having some problems remembering all the information on different accounts, all the people associated with different accounts and different brokers, and just remembering "who said what to whom, and when they said it." I don't think anyone noticed any problems, but I began worrying that maybe there was something wrong because I think my mother had Alzheimer's disease and, I am not sure, but I think one of her sisters had it as well. I didn't say anything to anyone, even my husband, and I was getting along okay, but I continued to feel that my memory was getting worse even though I must have read two dozen books on how to improve your memory. I also tried gingko biloba, which I bought and kept in the glove compartment of my car so that no one at home or at work would know I was taking it. I learned a number of helpful memory tricks and I still use those today but the gingko didn't seem to help, so I stopped taking it after about six or seven months. I still had the feeling that my memory was getting worse, but I was doing fine at work until just a couple weeks before I met you when I had just a terrible week. I called one broker who I know very well Elaine when her name is Eileen, and entirely confused a quote I was given on one account with a quote I was given on another. This led to a very embarrassing situation in which, for the first time, my boss looked at me as if he had serious doubts about my abilities. I went home in tears that day and told my husband what had happened and told him that I really thought I was developing Alzheimer's disease like my mother. My husband told me that he thought that was ridiculous and that it was I who was continuously reminding him of everything from appointments to the names of our friend's children. I actually felt better after I talked to him and when you told me that memory loss is normal, even in the forties and fifties, I felt even better. As we agreed, I had a really, really complete physical examination and the doctor found nothing wrong with me that he thought had anything to do with memory.

T.C.:   So, now, what has been your experience over the past three months taking the N-PEP-12 product that I gave you?

J.M.: Well, I really think it has helped a lot. I feel that my memory is sharper or quicker and I think my problem in confusing accounts and people with one another has almost vanished. I think I also feel happier and more confident because I am not always doubting myself or questioning myself. Before, if I picked up the phone and someone said hello, I would be very hesitant to use that person's name for fear that I'd be confusing him with someone else. I think other people in the office began to think that I was unfriendly because I would not immediately call them by name. I had to sort of rehearse the name in my head a couple of times before I spoke to be sure I wouldn't call someone by the wrong name. I also am more confident with information on each of my accounts and don't feel I have to read a reread and then reread again, all documents to be sure I am not making a mistake. So, I don't know if am doing a lot better because of N-PEP-12 or something else, but I certainly feel that my memory has improved and I feel much more confident now.

T.C.: So, do you intend to keep taking N-PEP-12?

J.M.: Oh my goodness, yes. In fact, I have gotten to the point where I am kind of hoarding boxes to be sure I don't run out.

T.C.: Well thanks so much for telling us about your experience. I think there are many people who can relate to the sort of memory problems that you experienced.

I suppose other N-PEP-12 products will be introduced in the future. I also suspect other products for memory developed through advanced biotechnology techniques will appear in coming years. For the moment though, N-PEP-12 stands alone against products for AAMI that are of greater historic than current interest.

6

Understanding Thoughts and Memories:

Improve Your Mood, Build Your Confidence and Sleep More Easily

In an earlier chapter I mentioned B.F. Skinner and described him as "arguably" the most influential psychologist of the twentieth century. Professor Skinner, though, was not at all concerned with thoughts. He and his many followers focused entirely on behavior. Indeed, they were and are known as "behaviorists" or "behavioral psychologists." Their focus was on "shaping" people through "operant conditioning" to perform desired tasks. A fundamental principle of operant conditioning is simply that any behavior followed by a reward is likely to be repeated. In fact, "behavior modification" programs based on operant conditioning can work remarkably well in parenting, in school systems, in corporate settings and in modifying undesirable behaviors.

At about the same time I met and briefly worked with Dr. Skinner, I met Dr. Aaron T. Beck, a psychiatrist and probably the most influential psychotherapist of the second half of the twentieth century. Dr. Beck is the father of Cognitive Behavioral Therapy (CBT), which has repeatedly been shown effective in treating depression, anxiety and a wide range of psychological disorders. Drs. Skinner and Beck share some common ground in that both taught the importance of behavioral interventions but, beyond that, CBT focuses on the thoughts that one has and the importance of those thoughts in subsequent feelings and behaviors, while behaviorists ignore thoughts altogether.

For example, both would agree that the first step in dealing with a depressed patient who sleeps twenty-two hours each day is to get the patient up and functioning for increasingly long periods each day. Beyond that, Behavior Modification and CBT have little in common, although both can be extremely useful in psychotherapy or in dealing with one's own life.

In the late 1970s I was trained by Dr. Beck and his colleagues at the University of Pennsylvania in the fundamentals of CBT and went on to practice variations on CBT techniques for years after that. It became apparent to me that information each of us stores in and retrieves from memory has an overwhelming effect on our mood, our reaction to the world around us and our perception of ourselves and others. A fundamental tenet of CBT is that emotions do not arise spontaneously, but are preceded by thoughts. Most people are not aware of this association and must train themselves to identify the thoughts that lead to feelings or, if you like, emotions. We all, though, have had the experience of suddenly feeling uneasy, or uncomfortable, or perhaps even happy and knowing that something made us feel that way, although we can't exactly remember what. If, every time you have such a strong feeling or emotion, you try very hard to recall the thought that went through your mind just prior to the emotion arising, you will eventually come to identify the thoughts that precede different feelings almost automatically. Sometimes these thoughts will come from interactions you are having at the moment, but more often they will come from memory and distorted thoughts from memory can cause depression, anxiety, loss of self-esteem, hostility and many other unproductive emotions.

Let me illustrate this relationship with several examples.

Elizabeth

Elizabeth, was an attractive, although somewhat disheveled and downcast, thirty-four-year-old woman who came to me complaining of depression, sleeplessness, loss of appetite and what amounted to anhedonia—that is, the inability to derive pleasure from any source. She continued to function adequately as an attorney, but had moved among three law firms and was convinced she would never be made a partner, which was said to be one of her principle goals in life. Another goal was to marry and have children, but she had no prospects of marriage and, indeed, all her affectional relations with males in recent years had been superficial and unrewarding. Elizabeth also reported no female friends outside her family and listed her mother, two sisters, and their three children as her family. Her father, who left the family when Elizabeth was eight years of age, and several aunts and uncles operated on the periphery of her life. In therapy, Elizabeth described herself as someone who had failed at everything and was a "loser" in life.

In CBT, the therapist does not argue or try to refute a point, but helps the patient test her thoughts and beliefs. So we began by having Elizabeth list all her major failures in life and all her major accomplishments. She quickly filled the list with twenty-five major failures, but could think of nothing to list on the positive side. She looked at me with tears welling up and said "See, this proves I am a loser." She responded to my prodding about significant accomplishments by disqualifying every possibility I listed. To the question "How about graduating from law school?" she answered: " It wasn't exactly Harvard" and "My grandfather worked his way through law school while taking care of his whole family; I didn't even pay my own tuition." In a similar manner, when I questioned whether Elizabeth's failure to be assigned to the perceived brightest third grade class, together with her friends, could properly be listed as a major failure in life twenty-five years later, she argued "You weren't there, you don't know what it felt like on the first day of school."

Let us examine, even at this early point, a few of the cognitive errors (or errors in thinking) that Elizabeth was making and that were likely associated with her feelings of depression and worthlessness. The first, quite common, error is *selective recall,* in which she readily recalled negative events, but blocked or failed to recall information that would contradict her negative beliefs. Second, when contradictory evidence was presented to her, she *disqualified information* that is in memory, with little regard for logic. Third, Elizabeth was engaged in *black and white thinking,* so that any evidence in memory that she is not a complete success must mean that she is a complete failure. And, fourth, she used *pejorative labeling* (i.e., loser) that further reinforced her negative thoughts about herself. Such labeling lends itself to automatic negative thoughts that can arise when one faces challenges (i.e., "You are a loser, you can't handle this problem.").

CBT is brief and targeted psychotherapy, so Elizabeth and I set out a six-week program with one visit per week, but a lot of "homework." We also set very specific goals. Bearing in mind that her two principal long-term goals in life related to her career and to marriage and family, we focused first on interpersonal skills that would be important in both cases. We focused initially on the workplace, because this was the arena in which she was active, while most of her time away from work was spent alone. It was apparent from our conversation that Elizabeth's negative thoughts extended beyond her self-evaluation to include her views of her colleagues, her law firm, her home and the world in general. We spoke about this negative world view and the effect it might have on her life and, although Elizabeth believed the negativity was the result of many bad experiences and that it was "not the other way around," she agreed to a three-week experiment to test the idea.

Elizabeth first completed several rating scales measuring her mood, satisfaction with life, quality of interpersonal relationships and other aspects of psychological well being. We then agreed that for the first week of the test period she would begin monitoring her thoughts and record as many of these thoughts as possible. She would list the time and place each thought occurred and would also identify the feeling that followed each thought. She would also rate the discomfort associated with each feeling on a scale from 1 to 7.

Elizabeth was dutiful and came to our second meeting with five yellow legal pads filled with literally hundreds of negative thoughts and associated feelings. As I expected, she was flooded with negative thoughts in the evening, when she was alone, and particularly when she lay in bed attempting to fall asleep. These thoughts were drawn from memories of the day's events and memories of other events going all the way back to early childhood. We examined the thoughts and feelings; looked for common themes, common times, settings or circumstances in which thoughts arose; and identified the thoughts associated with the most painful feelings.

In this second session, I gained from Elizabeth two important, albeit tentative, admissions: first, that she had many more negative thoughts than she realized and, second, that there might be some association between these thoughts and her feelings of depression and unhappiness.

In Week 2 of the program, Elizabeth continued to monitor her thoughts and feelings, but we added another condition. That was, do not automatically accept these thoughts; we will test their validity later and, most important, do not let these thoughts affect your interactions with others. In fact, I instructed, say nothing negative to others—no matter what negative thoughts arose. Instead, I recommended that she substitute positive statements about the other individual if at all possible. She was to list each such statement and the feeling (and intensity) that followed.

Elizabeth was, once again, dutiful. She arrived at our third session with reams of paper. Again, we examined common themes in the negative thoughts and began to test the evidence to support and refute each of the several very painful recurring thoughts.

By now, Elizabeth and I had formed a therapist-patient relationship and the solemnity and tears of the first session gave way to at least some humor as we tested the evidence to support her negative thoughts. We were able to list evidence on the refute side of the page in testing such thoughts as, "I have never been of any value to anyone" and "I have never accomplished anything important."

For the third and final week of the experiment, I taught Elizabeth the techniques of thought-blocking that I referred to earlier. One cultivates a positive memory in great detail and replaces negative thoughts and memories with it much as one would eject one DVD and insert another. We continued recording negative thoughts and now monitored the success of the thought blocking technique in terms of percentage from 0 to 100%.

It is important that people such as Elizabeth who engage in black and white thinking, learn to think in degrees of success or failure, sadness or happiness, pain and pleasure so that, for example, one flaw or even many flaws in oneself or one's marriage does not mean that one is a "loser" or that her marriage is a "disaster." We also continued the practice of avoiding negative statements or behavior and substituting positive statements, about the individual one is addressing and others, if possible.

At the end of the three-week experiment, at her fourth visit to my office, I had Elizabeth again complete the same self-rating forms she completed before we began the experiment. We had already agreed in writing that a change in scores would be the test of whether our experiment had succeeded or failed. In fact, Elizabeth reported significantly less severe symptoms of depression, greater satisfaction with life and better interpersonal relations. To be sure, Elizabeth was still reporting levels on all these scales associated with dysphoria, or mild depression, but she had improved quite significantly in only three weeks. So, we agreed to continue this approach to therapy for three additional weeks and we devoted the remainder of the session to examining the thoughts and feelings recorded in the previous week and Elizabeth's attempts to block or address the negative thoughts.

One of thought-evoking episodes we focused on had occurred several days earlier when a coworker, who Elizabeth regarded as clever and witty, invited Elizabeth to join her and another coworker for lunch. Elizabeth was caught off-guard by the invitation and declined, saying that she had too much work to do. She was then overcome by a series of negative thoughts including: "She must feel sorry for me because I always eat alone in my office"; "I can't go because I would have nothing to talk about"; "I don't want anyone to know how boring my life is, I am a complete loser"; "I should have gone, I never do the right thing"; "This is so embarrassing that I will have to find another job" ; and "They are probably talking about me right now about how pathetic I am."

Elizabeth listed each of these thoughts and recorded very high levels of "sadness" associated with each. She did, however, attempt to list evidence to support and refute each thought. To the first thought, for example, she was able to provide the refutation "Well, even if that is true, it just means they want to help me," and to the last thought she provided the refutation "They are both very nice, and funny and never seem to say anything nasty about anyone." Elizabeth was able to note the "black and white thought" error in "I never do the right thing" and refute that she usually does do the right thing. As we had discussed previously, she also noted that cognitive error in "I am a complete loser."

We also discussed the importance of the word *"should"* in negative thoughts and how that must always be questioned. I noted that there are advantages and disadvantages to almost any course of action and "should" often irrationally argues against weighing the two sides.

Finally, from this one episode, we discussed another cognitive error that appeared in Elizabeth's thinking and may have caused problems in her life earlier. That is the problem of catastrophic thinking. We see it here in the thought that "This is so embarrassing that I will have to find another job." In *catastrophic thinking,* one greatly exaggerates the negative consequences of an action or of failing to have taken an action. This is quite a common cognitive error and we should all be on guard against it. In this case, Elizabeth had taken a simple decline of a casual lunch invitation and turned it into a life-changing crisis. When we examined the reasons why she left her two previous law firms, we noted that catastrophic thinking had played a clear role in one case and a probable role in another.

Going into the fourth week of therapy we continued the thought monitoring process and added some behavioral interventions, in addition to the positive verbal statements already in effect. First, Elizabeth would seek out the two coworkers who had invited her to lunch and would reciprocate the invitation. She would carefully monitor her thoughts and feelings leading up to issuing the invitation and try to address or block negative thoughts and this process would continue through the event if the invitation were accepted. Also, I noted that I could see the change in her face since we had begun therapy—she smiled now when there had been no sign of a smile three weeks earlier. Also, she no longer looked as is she were about to break out into tears, and no longer looked disheveled and at wit's end, as she did in our first meeting. We decided that, in the coming week, Elizabeth would try on at least five occasions each day to smile at a coworker even though there was no smile or pleasant word from the individual.

I learned a week later that the luncheon invitation was accepted and, despite Elizabeth's doubts, the three women had a great deal in common and Elizabeth indicated she laughed more than at any time since she had been in college. Of course there was no shortage of negative thoughts during the week, but Elizabeth was becoming very good at recognizing the thoughts that preceded feelings and testing those thoughts logically.

In the remaining two weeks of therapy we worked further on examining the cognitive errors that were associated with Elizabeth's depression and attendant problems with sleep and appetite. She learned to examine the long-held memories associated with her feelings of worthlessness and, perhaps more important, to build and continuously expand a library of intricate positive memories from earlier life that could be called upon to refute negative thoughts. Indeed, there was no shortage at all of such memories in Elizabeth's life. She had loving parents, despite an acrimonious divorce, wonderful grandparents, she was an excellent student throughout her school and university years and was once an enthusiastic, if not overwhelmingly talented, musician and athlete.

What led Elizabeth to develop cognitive problems such as selective remembering and subsequent depression is largely unknown and likely to remain so. There are experiences in all lives to which damage can be attributed, but it is not necessary, or perhaps even important, to discover what caused cognitive problems and led to psychopathology. It is far more valuable to deal with negative and unproductive thoughts, whatever their cause.

I spoke with Elizabeth about two months after our therapy sessions and, for the first time in years she was regularly dating a fellow attorney and was almost giddy with excitement. I cautioned her that, like negative emotions, positive emotions are preceded by thoughts and it is important to examine the likely accuracy of these thoughts. I suggested that a thought such as "This man will give me everything I have always longed for in life" can be just as damaging as the negative thoughts we dealt with in therapy.

It is, perhaps, not surprising that Elizabeth did not call again. When one is besotted, rationality is often suspended and that is why the entirely different views of reality provided by parties in divorce proceedings give rise to such intense negative emotions. But I have always hoped that Elizabeth went on to a wonderful and happy life based on her ability to test the rational basis of thoughts that arise from memory.

Vincent

Vincent was a fifty-two-year-old executive who was "a hail fellow well met" by any standard that I know. He scheduled a meeting with me on the Monday following his return with his wife from the college graduation ceremony of his youngest son. In distinct contrast to Elizabeth, Vincent seemed to be interconnected to friends and acquaintances throughout the world. He was a member of seemingly dozens of professional and fraternal groups and counted renowned individuals among his friends. Vincent had married his college sweetheart almost thirty years earlier and, by his account, had an ideal wife and family, and was at the top of his game professionally.

I listened to Vincent's accounts of his friends and exploits for most of our fifty minute session without commenting or showing signs that I had either positive or negative thoughts about his accounts. With fewer than fifteen minutes remaining and trying to be polite, I interrupted Vincent and asked why he had come to see me. He stopped in mid-sentence, looked down at his chair in silence, looked up at me with tears in his eyes and said, "because I don't know if I want to live any longer." I responded by asking simply "How would you like me to help you with that decision?" Vincent responded very slowly and said, "I don't know, but at least I am glad I told someone." We agreed that we would meet the following week, Vincent would tell me what service he wanted from me, and I would tell him if I thought I could provide that service.

The tone of our meeting the following week was entirely businesslike, with no braggadocio and no tears. The first issue on my agenda was assessment of suicide risk. One must take references to suicide quite seriously, in general, but particularly when made by a middle-aged or older male. They tend to use means such as guns that are quite lethal and the ratio of successful to threatened suicides is very high. What one looks for in assessing suicide, among other factors, is whether the individual is hopeless—that is, he sees no possibility that his present situation will improve—and how far along he is in planning the event. At the final stages of planning, one will often have worked out not only the means of suicide and the place, but also exactly what the room will look like when the body is found, who will find the body, what each family member and friend will think, and so on.

As I expected, in Vincent's case, planning wasn't too far beyond making the event look like an accident, and the threatened act did not appear imminent. We rationally examined what would be gained (freedom from acting like someone he was not) and lost (not knowing grandchildren, causing pain to family, religious doubts, etc.) and Vincent acknowledged that the books did not balance on the side of suicide, particularly if another means could be found to ease the psychic pain he was feeling.

We began a discussion of the services Vincent expected of me and he told me that he certainly didn't think he was "crazy," but he had worked himself into a very serious predicament and he did not know how to escape. He could not discuss the matter with family or friends because that would mean revealing what only he knew to be true. He didn't even want to reveal the problem to a psychologist in the city where he lived, and he flew in to see me after reading an article that quoted me in a newspaper. He told me he simply wished to hear my thoughts on his situation and help him examine how he could escape. The problem, he related, was that he was seen by everyone he knew as being something he was not. He was, he indicated, a "phony." He was seen by everyone he knew as being a successful businessman, a well informed and smart advisor, a great dinner companion and golfing buddy, a generous contributor to charities, and a great husband and father. He acknowledged some merit to the perception that he was a good husband and father, but aside from that everything was false and, in fact, when his wife and children learned the truth, they would be ashamed of him too.

Already, you should have learned an important point from Vincent's case. That is, do not feel confident that you know what someone thinks of himself based on how he behaves, what he tells you, or what others think of him. In Vincent's case, as well as in cases of celebrated men such as Ernest Hemingway (who was a patient of Dr. Beck before he developed CBT), there was a powerful recurring thought that he was a "phony" who would eventually be discovered, and with whom no one would even associate when the true Vincent was known. Yet nothing in Vincent's words or manner portrayed that to me, and Vincent acknowledged that even his wife had no idea what he was thinking.

Vincent readily acknowledged critical memories that supported his thoughts of being a "phony." Vincent was oldest son in a family of five children. His mother was described as never working outside the home and being a generally benign woman. The father, by contrast, was described as an alcoholic and an angry and brutal man who frequently berated his wife and children, particularly Vincent. The verbal attacks on Vincent were often accompanied by violent physical attacks that were said to be entirely unprovoked on many occasions. The father was an often-unemployed auto mechanic who sometimes performed repairs in the backyard of the home that Vincent's impoverished family happened to be living in at the moment. On such occasions, beginning when he was six or eight years old, Vincent would be called upon to assist his father. Such assistance at first involved finding a particular tool or holding a flashlight, and progressed over the years to more difficult tasks that Vincent would be told to perform with little or no instruction. When almost inevitable difficulties arose, Vincent's father would scream, often within hearing range of neighbors, a series of profanities ending in "You better learn to make a living with words, boy, because you will never make it with your hands; you are worthless to me," or some slight variation thereof. On a daily basis, his father demonstrated values as well as skills that were valuable to him, and these included attacking any potential foe "before he attacks you," "never be a brown noser," "tell it like it is," "never be a phony," and so on.

As Vincent moved through school, he came to think that not only was he not good with his hands, but he was not very good in most academic subjects either. He could conceal this in some subjects by working extreme hours on homework and acting as if he had spent only a few minutes. He also learned that his most important asset in getting through school was having friends who would help him, often without even recognizing they were doing so. In high school, and particularly in college, he learned that he could form groups or committees of smarter students and take much of the credit for their work. He carried this same strategy into his first job and realized that he could function within an industry he didn't understand very well by making the right friends and depending upon them for advice and assistance. In return for this help, Vincent reported that he learned on an individual basis how easy it is to help people feel better about themselves without ever appearing to be ingratiating. In other words, he understood the relationship between thoughts and feelings and was practicing a form of CBT for his own advancement.

Vincent reported that as years passed and he rose steadily in his industry he felt more and more "over his head." He stated that he "knew he had to get off the train" at some point before his lack of technical knowledge was revealed, as he thought it nearly had been on several occasions. The point of departure he chose several years earlier was the graduation from college of his youngest son, and his consequent release from a significant financial burden.

I asked Vincent about the feelings he was experiencing at the moment and the thoughts that preceded those feelings and he said, "mostly relief" and "I guess as I tell the story out loud it doesn't sound quite as bad as when I think about it." And I continued, "Particularly at night?", to which Vincent responded that this was the worst time for his negative thoughts. And here is a second general point to learn from Vincent's case: do not lie in bed at night, unable to sleep, thinking about your life and your problems. This is the time when you will generally experience the most negative thoughts and are least able to accurately test them. So get back out of bed if you cannot sleep and occupy your mind with reading or other activities and go back to bed only when you are almost sure you can fall asleep.

As our session was nearing its end, I asked Vincent to monitor his thoughts and feelings in the coming week and to provide me next week with *his* definition of the word "phony," not a dictionary definition. Finally, I asked him to list the questions he could be asked that would most clearly reveal his lack of technical knowledge and describe the likely outcomes if that were to happen.

Vincent appeared for our third meeting with all his tasks accomplished and apparently ready for business. He first provided the five technical questions that would bring about his downfall and each struck me as very highly technical, particularly when the consequences of his failure to answer correctly were said to be catastrophic, both personally and for his company. I asked him the probability of a security analyst or a large stockholder asking the first question on the list and, after at first refusing to set a probability, finally settled on 10%. I then asked him the question, as if I were an analyst or investor, and he gave me a highly technical answer that sounded completely reasonable to me, but Vincent assured me it was superficial.

We discussed the need to think probabilistically rather than in black and white terms, and examined whether the catastrophic outcomes Vincent imagined were highly probable, particularly since he worked for a large publicly traded company that was not about to collapse because a single employee made an uninformed comment.

We then examined his list of thoughts and feelings during the week and noted the frequent thoughts related to being phony, hiding his "stupidity," and "becoming a "laughingstock" among younger executives and so on. As one would expect these thoughts were often accompanied by what Vincent abbreviated as "S,'" meaning "that sick feeling you get as a kid when you get in trouble."

We examined rational ways to address many of Vincent's thoughts. For example, Vincent acknowledged that many of the younger executives who he feared would laugh at him had, in fact, worked very hard for his approval and in many cases had been recruited by him. I also asked Vincent if he thought others at the company and within the industry were so obtuse that they had no idea of the limits of his technical knowledge. He indicated that they must not know or he would not still be in his job.

I asked if we could test whether Vincent's technical knowledge was accurately perceived within the company. Was there someone, for example, who Vincent trusted and who he could confide in on this matter? He initially answered in the negative, but finally agreed he would consider discussing the matter with his former mentor who had retired to a ranch in Wyoming. We calculated the worst possible outcome of such a call and the probability that it would occur and Vincent agreed the risk was acceptable. The session had by now come to an end and we agreed to keep monitoring and testing thoughts and to postpone the discussion of the word "phony" and other pejorative terms that arose in Vincent's mind until the following week.

In fact, Vincent called me the following afternoon, fully back into his hale-fellow persona. He related that his mentor had responded to his concerns with "Vinnie, you are the best strategist in the business and a fantastic team leader and consensus builder in the company. Nobody in the business sees you as some kind of super technician. You know enough to understand the big picture, and that is all that is important at your level." So, just as neither I, nor apparently anyone else, read the thoughts on Vincent's mind, neither was he a mind reader and his attempt to do so caused him long and serious pain.

In our fourth and, as it turned out, final meeting, Vincent and I examined the word "phony," and the other pejorative words and images that arose in his thoughts and led to feelings of anxiety, dysphoria and even a sick feeling deep in his chest and stomach. We discussed how his father's need to clash with others had served him so poorly in life, whereas Vincent's diplomacy and interpersonal skills had served him so well. We examined each of the definitions of "phony" that Vincent had developed and decided that a better word would be "diplomat" or "big picture guy." Similarly, we created definitions for "strategist," "team leader," and "consensus builder," and we agreed that Vincent was all these things. Indeed, we concluded that our definitions of these terms were very much consistent with how Vincent's father would have defined his pejorative terms.

We then practiced the exercise of—DVD-like—ejecting his father's old pejorative words when they arose and substituting Vincent's new more positive words which, after all, described the very same behaviors so hated by his father. We agreed that no further meetings were necessary, but that Vincent was welcome to call me if further problems arose. As in the earlier sessions, he paid in cash, presumably so there would be no record of his having consulted a psychologist. I never heard from him again.

As a therapist, I could interpret this as meaning that Vincent had greatly benefited from our sessions and worked his way out of his predicament, or that he did not find my approach helpful and took another course. A brief examination of the arguments supporting each interpretation led me to accept the former, as you will gather from the observation that we are discussing this case years later.

Barbara

I met Barbara when she was forty-three years old and in the midst of divorce proceedings after almost twenty years of marriage. Barbara had worked for an advertising agency that her husband had formed years earlier, but she resigned when her husband suggested a marital separation. That occurred about five months earlier and Barbara was currently working in temporary administrative jobs. She had two adolescent children, a daughter and a son, who lived with her in the family home. Aside from her contact with them, she had retreated from social interaction outside of her ever-changing workplace. Barbara came to my office complaining of memory problems, sadness, and extreme fatigue. She appeared sad and worn, she avoided eye contact, and spoke in a monotone. While her attire was appropriate, it seemed a size or two too small. Her family physician sent her for evaluation of the memory problems and had suggested antidepressant and sedative hypnotic medication, but medication was rejected by Barbara. There was no evidence of memory loss upon objective psychological testing and her psychological complaints were suggestive of depression.

I agreed to see Barbara for two or three sessions following the initial evaluation and was intrigued that, like Elizabeth, she suffered from the cognitive error *selective recall*. Unlike Elizabeth, however, she selectively recalled *positive* aspects of her married life and her husband's behavior. She said that the divorce was entirely her fault because she had failed to notice how her husband had grown and, thus, she had not met his new needs.

Barbara indicated that she knew that she would never be happy again without her husband, but that she did not want medication because she did not want to be dependent on drugs and she just had to learn to live without "the only man I could ever love." Barbara indicated that her husband was seven years older than she and that she had met him in searching for a job just after graduation from college. I asked if she had been generally happy during childhood, adolescence and her college years and she answered yes, she had a great life and was almost always happy. For the remainder of the session I discussed the relationship between thoughts and feelings and, as with Elizabeth and Vincent, asked her to monitor her thoughts and feelings in writing in the coming weeks. I also asked her to list in writing her ten greatest strengths and weaknesses and to describe in writing the ten happiest memories in her life before meeting her husband.

Barbara appeared for the next session looking and acting slightly more upbeat than in the earlier session and her scores on a depression rating scale and satisfaction with life rating scale were slightly improved over a week earlier. She began by saying "You have given me a lot to think about," and as we began to examine her recorded thoughts and subsequent feelings it became apparent that she, like many people, confused thoughts with feelings. I explained that she didn't "feel" that her husband didn't care for her anymore. That was a thought, and it may be followed by any feeling from sadness to anger to indifference, depending upon what one expects or desires from the other person. Nevertheless, one could see that the vast majority of her negative thoughts focused on her husband's rejection. Subsequent feelings would most appropriately have been labeled "sad," "worthless," "stupid," and so on. It seemed from Barbara's notes that negative thoughts were most likely to occur in the evening when she was relaxing with a glass of wine and, particularly, when she played her favorite recordings, many of which she had listened to with her husband. Thoughts were also associated with seeing her husband's picture and his clothes and possessions, many of which were left in the house when he left five months earlier.

We then turned to the list of Barbara's ten greatest strengths and weaknesses. It will not be surprising that the list of weaknesses was glaring and consistent with the recurring negative thoughts. There were also, physical references to being "fat," "ugly," and "old looking." By contrast, the list of strengths diminished after "used to be a good mother" to important but not overwhelming attributes such as "always on time." We moved on then to the description of Barbara's happiest memories before meeting her husband. Here, her mood palpably changed. We focused on one memory first, a one-week trip to Ocean City, Maryland with her parents, siblings, uncles, aunts, cousins and other family members when Barbara was thirteen years old. I asked her to close her eyes and tell me everything she remembered about the trip. She went into such great detail with this single memory, smiling as she related details, that the whole session might have been taken up with this happy bit of nostalgia. We reviewed several of the other memories and there was no evidence of cognitive distortions.

At this point it was clear to me that Barbara's cognitive distortions were almost entirely limited to her husband. It was her thoughts associated with him that we had to challenge. With fifteen minutes left in the session, I asked a key question: "Barbara, you told me that you could never be happy without your husband, but we see here that you were very happy before you met him. You were not miserable, as you describe yourself now, so isn't it possible that you could be happy without him again?" "I don't think so," she responded, "he has been my soulmate and partner since I was just a girl." "But he is not your partner now, and you told me you see no chance of reconciliation," I responded and then continued: "You may be right; you may be unhappy for the rest of your life, no matter what you do, but I am asking whether you want to test the possibility that you can be happy without your husband, as you once were." Barbara agreed to a two week test of the idea and again completed the depression and quality of life rating scales. Her "homework" was as follows:

1. Continue monitoring thoughts and feelings in writing.
2. Remove all pictures of your husband that you can without upsetting the children. Certainly remove all his pictures from your bedroom.
3. Store all your husband's clothes and possessions in the garage or basement.
4. Replace the music you listen to with music that does not remind you of your husband, particularly, Gloria Gaynor's "I Will Survive."
5. Begin to remodel your bedroom as you like it. Buy new bedclothes if you can.
6. Practice and enhance the wonderful memories you talked about today. Form five fully developed CDs in your mind, put

labels on them and be ready to insert one when you begin to think of your husband and remember good times together.

7. Form a picture in your mind of your husband looking angry and disdainful, or imagine what he looked like at a time he was least attractive to you. When positive images of your husband arise in your mind, immediately substitute this image. Practice so that the image comes readily to mind.

The following week Barbara arrived looking much happier, but she first told me that she had cried all week, whereupon she immediately began to cry. She told me her feelings vacillated during the week from the best she had felt in five months to the saddest. She reported, and indicated in her thought monitoring papers, that she felt as she had when her father died five years earlier. When she moved her husband's things to the basement it was if she were burying him, she said. I responded by asking whether it was possible that similar feelings could arise because similar thoughts were going through her mind? We turned in Barbara's notes to the days on which these feelings of overwhelming sadness and loss occurred and she, in fact, had listed the thoughts: "I will never be with him again," "I will always love him," and "I will always miss him"— probably the same thoughts, she acknowledged, that drove the depression she felt upon the death of her father. As we discussed these thoughts, Barbara acknowledged that she would, of course, see the husband again. After all, he was the father of her children and remained a dutiful father. She also acknowledged that although she might "always" love and miss her husband, she had already learned from her father's death that the pain would diminish very significantly with time. Further review of her "homework" revealed that Barbara had, in fact, removed most reminders of her husband and had tried the recommended thought-blocking techniques with some success. Although she had been overwhelmed at times during the week, she had succeeded on many occasions in blocking negative thoughts and, almost certainly, preventing many such thoughts from arising.

I decided to devote the remainder of the session to the saintly husband and began by having Barbara list the husband's strengths and weaknesses just as she had listed her own. As expected, the list of strengths could have been taken from requirements to sit as a knight at King Arthur's court while weaknesses listed were petty and trivial. So, it was time to have an objective look at this wonderful fellow. Review of the marital history with Barbara revealed that the husband had wide mood swings and that he was capable of being both a loving and supportive husband and a depressed, angry mate who would berate and diminish Barbara. As the years had gone on, the percentage of time in the latter state was estimated by Barbara as thirty percent, whereas it was said to be near zero in the first years of marriage and to have grown steadily after that. He also appeared to be a philanderer and, while Barbara could confirm two sexual affairs, she had probable cause to believe that many others had occurred. Also, while the family income had been more than adequate to sustain an upper-middle class lifestyle, the husband lived just on the edge of what his income would support. There were minimal savings and substantial bills and when sacrifices were required to pay the monthly bills, they were often made by Barbara or the children. I will not go beyond that but, let us say, that the husband's behavior had been something less than perfectly consistent with the words chosen by Barbara.

We then examined whether, for example, the sexual trysts were consistent with the word "devoted" she had chosen in listing the husband's strengths. Or, was "supportive" consistent with the not uncommon berating Barbara described? Was "good provider" consistent with passing off financial sacrifices to one's wife and children?

At the end of the session, I reminded Barbara that we were in the midst of a two-week experiment to examine her contention that she could never be happy without her husband. I asked her to at least examine the possibility that the ideal husband that she could not live without was one that never existed in reality. Could it be one she created in her memory by selectively recalling and magnifying positive attributes and experiences and blocking out those memories that were inconsistent? Barbara agreed to at least consider the proposition and to continue the cognitive techniques she was mastering. I also told her that I wanted her to take up an activity outside the home that would be good for her physically, that would leave her with less idle time for negative thoughts to intrude and that would put her in contact with other people. She told me that "It is funny that you say that because I have gained so much weight and I am determined to lose at least some of it." That is, of course, what I hoped she would say.

The fourth and final session was marked by a very clear improvement in Barbara's reported mood and satisfaction with life. We reviewed her thoughts and feelings for the week, we tested a few of the thoughts but, clearly, Barbara had learned to test thoughts logically on her own. She had used several of the thought-blocking techniques she had developed and avoided the situations most likely to evoke negative thoughts. The nightmare scenario in this case would be sitting alone at home with a glass of wine, listening to Barry Manilow records while thumbing through the family photo album. Barbara had also spoken to her mother and sister about the possibility that she had attributed to her husband qualities that were not apparent to others. Both readily agreed and carried the argument further saying that many of these attributes were not apparent to Barbara either before the divorce. They reminded her of the many conversations they had with each other about their husbands and families and Barbara's frequent complaints about her husband being away, about money, and about his berating and suspicious behavior.

Barbara agreed that she probably had modified her husband's attributes in memory and that she would examine thoughts that arose about him and test them logically. Finally, Barbara had joined a health club and was determined to lose twenty pounds by Memorial Day, the beginning of summer at the beach in the Northeast and then about four months away.

I received Christmas cards with notes from Barbara after our sessions together and noted a name change after three or four years. A photograph of the new family was enclosed and Barbara looked very happy, indeed.

All-in-All

So, you see, memory is not just about names, appointments or where your eyeglasses are residing at the moment. It is the basis of who you believe you are and how you feel about yourself and others. It is the basis of your confidence, or lack thereof, and the extent to which you are happy or sad. When you are alone, your memories can be your best friends who will lull you to sleep and put a smile on your face. They can also be your worst enemies when they become negative and destructive and run amok. Distorted memories can undermine your confidence, keep you awake at night, induce depression and anxiety, and ruin your life. Fortunately, you can learn to bring dark thoughts and memories out into the sunshine of logic and crystal clear thought.

If you wish to know more about CBT, I suggest you look for one of the brilliant books of Dr. David Burns, a psychiatrist and early student of Dr. Beck. Try his book, *Feeling Good: The New Mood Therapy*. It has sold over three million copies and you will find it extremely interesting.

7

The Memory Advantage

We are all competitors in one way or another, and most of us have a reasonably clear idea of the physical, psychological and interpersonal strengths and weaknesses that allow us to compete with others. Shy, retiring people usually realize that they are not cut out to be salesman; hyperactive people who have trouble concentrating on a single topic or object for more than a few seconds generally do not choose to compete in the workplace as air traffic controllers; and short guys who are great in math rarely choose playing in the National Basketball Association as a promising career path. There are some abilities, though, that come into play in almost all arenas in which we might choose to compete, and one of these is memory. Whether one is a salesman, air traffic controller, basketball player, or in any other field of endeavor, memory is critical to acquiring required skills, as well as maintaining, sharpening and refining those skills over the years.

Beyond that, as we have seen, we all define who we are based on our memories of earlier life and these memories can make us confident, or filled with self-doubt; happy and productive, or miserable and disabled; relaxed and easygoing or chronically anxious and always on the edge of disaster. Thus, aside from remembering and refining the specific skills of an occupation or endeavor, positive and supportive memories can give an individual a tremendous competitive advantage in almost any undertaking in life.

In preceding chapters I hope you have learned about the basic neurophysiology of memory, about "normal" age-related changes in memory and how these compare with early signs of a dementing disorder such as AD, and about the many factors that can cause memory problems at any age. In Chapter 3, I reminded you of the importance of diet, exercise, stress reduction, adequate sleep, smoking cessation, avoidance of problematic drugs used to treat medical or psychiatric disorders, and the general observation that what is good for your heart is good for your brain. This information will be found in many books about memory and establishes the groundwork for *The Memory Advantage.* Here we depart from the advice of other authors, though, and consider what is novel about *The Memory Advantage.*

First, ***The Value of Forgetting***. It is neither desirable nor healthy to develop a "photographic memory." Your brain is designed to screen out the vast, vast majority of information that comes to you via your eyes, ears, nose, and skin. It is designed to sort through this mass of information and exclude from entering even temporary stages of memory (e.g., working memory) all information that will not be adaptive in the future. When information is deemed extremely important for survival it is most likely to be remembered and memory storage is aided by chemicals released from critical brain centers such as the amygdala. Memory for such events (the collapse of the World Trade Center Towers, for example) is indelibly engraved in memory with no conscious effort.

Many people seek to overcome the natural screening process of the brain and perceptual systems and to remember all sorts of information that is quite unlikely to ever be adaptive in the future. That is much like keeping all the clothes you ever owned in your closet in the very unlikely chance that bell bottom pants, Nehru suits, or the once ubiquitous lime green polyester will return to the center of the fashion world. It is important to forget trivial events and also negative and painful memories that may serve no useful purpose. In fact, these latter memories may be highly maladaptive. In Chapter 4, I showed you a technique for blocking negative and harmful memories. As you practice this technique and make a conscious effort to exclude from memory information that is not adaptive, you will come to appreciate the value of forgetting.

Next, when you clearly want to remember something that you hope will be adaptive in the future (each reader can form his own image here) step one is to ***Pay Attention.*** The vast majority of the time when we do not remember the name of someone to whom we have been introduced, for example, it is because we didn't pay attention to the name when it was provided. We may have been thinking about our retort, what the person or others may think of us, the identity of the next person to be introduced and so on. On those relatively rare occasions in which you do want to enter information into long term memory, focus like a laser beam, and repeat the information out loud or over and over to yourself.

Paying attention is the first and absolutely essential step in memory, but bear in mind that the healthy brain filters out information that is not likely to be adaptive even if it does enter clearly into our consciousness. One way around this buffer is to *Associate* the new information with other information that is already in memory, having passed the adaptivity test previously. So, if I meet "Joan," I can compare her appearance with other Joans I know, *Visualize* her as Joan of Arc or in a Joan Crawford movie role, or form a mental image of her speaking on a phone, or of a clown-like cone on her head, and so on. The key is to tie Joan to information already in memory. If that can be done visually, the association will be strongest.

Next, in the words of the renowned psychologist B. F. Skinner, create a ***Prosthetic Memory Environment***. Or as Professor Skinner also argued "Rely on memos not memory." Professor Skinner used the term "memo" twenty-five years ago when devices to relieve us of many burdensome memory tasks were largely limited to note pads, refrigerator magnets, the ubiquitous Post-it Notes, and strings around the finger. Today many of us operate with Personal Data Assistants (PDAs) of one sort or another that seem absolutely essential. Arguments that have been made along the "use it or lose it" line—that it is better that we try to remember as much as possible rather than rely on such devices—are intuitively appealing, but scientifically weak (at least for the brain). In reality, we now have wonderful memory devices that can dramatically increase individual productivity at any age.

A key element of *The Memory Advantage* that you almost certainly have not heard of before is the nutraceutical product, or dietary supplement if you prefer that term, N-PEP-12. Other such products for memory have been available for decades, centuries, or even millennia, and most of the brand name products sold for memory improvement are simply mixtures of these same old ingredients, often at dosage levels that would be far too low, even is the individual ingredients in the product worked. N-PEP-12 is a product of state-of-the-art biotechnology that I recently found effective in treating normal, age-related memory loss. That study was published in an academic journal in 2005 and followed many failures in clinical trials that I conducted to find drugs and nutraceuticals effective in treating "normal" age-related memory loss.

Glucose is the primary source of energy in the brain and glucose availability diminishes during the normal aging process and after exposure to various neurological diseases, medical diseases, stress and other bodily insults. N-PEP-12 changes the availability of glucose in the brain at the DNA level by increasing the expression of a specific gene (Glut-1) that partially controls the passage of glucose into the brain.

Beyond the effects of N-PEP-12 on brain glucose are its critical effects on neuronal plasticity. We now know that memories are formed by growing new connections among neurons, and in some cases growing new neurons altogether. In the young developing brain there are abundant amounts of chemical nerve growth factor (NGF) to support neuronal and dendritic growth, but amounts are depleted in middle and later adult life and that diminution decreases brain plasticity. It is not possible to administer exogenous NGF because it does not cross the blood brain barrier (BBB). N-PEP-12, by contrast, does cross the BBB and mimics the effects of NGF, thereby increasing neuronal plasticity. This allows the older brain to grow new neurons and new interconnections among neurons and facilitates the formation of new memories.

Another element of *The Memory Advantage* that may be unique and that I consider extremely important is gaining an understanding of the relationship between memory, on the one hand, and mood, confidence, sleep and other aspects of human existence on the other. Feelings, whether happiness, sorrow, guilt, hatred, or love, do not arise spontaneously. They are preceded by thoughts, and often these thoughts are not based on what is happening to the individual at the moment but on memories. *Memories can be your warmest friends or your most bitter detractors.* In Chapter 6, I introduced you to the techniques of Cognitive Behavior Therapy and I argued that it is important for you to understand the relationship between the information you have stored in memory and how you think and feel every day. I gave you a technique for purging maladaptive memories and substituting some of the wonderful memories that you have accumulated over the course of a lifetime. These memories will help keep you strong and confident. Together with the steps outlined above, that is *The Memory Advantage* you will have wherever you choose to compete.

Readers with personal stories or thoughts can reach the author at tcrook@psychologix.com.

Glossary and Key Concepts

Acetylcholine: A neurotransmitter of critical importance for memory. Drugs that block or degrade this neurotransmitter can produce memory loss so profound as to resemble dementia when administered to healthy young adults. Some drugs that enhance acetylcholine levels can improve memory.

Acetyl L-Carnitine (ALC): Derived from carnitine, ALC is a naturally occurring substance in the human body. It has been sold as a drug for many years in Europe and, for the past twelve years, as a dietary supplement in the United States. ALC helps the body metabolize fatty acids for energy and is important for energy utilization in every cell in the body. ALC has been studied for the treatment of a very wide variety of conditions including weight loss and heart disease, as well as Alzheimer's disease. Results in AD are, at best, equivocal and there is no sound evidence that ALC is effective in AAMI or related disorders. Nevertheless, it is sold as a dietary supplement for improving memory Age-Associated Memory Impairment.

Age-Associated Memory Impairment (AAMI): A diagnostic term applied to persons fifty years or older who have experienced "normal" memory loss since they were young adults. Symptoms include problems remembering names, misplacing objects such as eyeglasses and keys, and forgetting tasks one intended to perform. AAMI is *not* a precursor of Alzheimer's disease.

Alzheimer's disease (AD): A dementing, dehabilitating disease of later life. Changes in the brain include deposition of a sticky

119

amyloid plaque and tangled neuronal structures in brain areas critical for memory.

Amygdala: A limbic structure found in the brain's temporal lobes, just in front of the hippocampus. This almond-shaped structure labeled the amygdala. The amygdala helps transfer information from short-term to long-term memory. The amygdala's main function seems to be linking memories that were formed through several senses and linking memories and emotions.

Amnesia: Loss of memory due to brain injury or disease.

Anticholingeric effects: The blocking or degrading of a neurotransmitter, often by drugs, the result of which is memory loss.

Antioxidants: Substances that block or inhibit destructive oxidation reactions, thus preventing the formation of dangerous free radicals, or that, after their formation, deactivate them. All living cells contain complex systems of antioxidant chemicals and enzymes to prevent chemical cellular damage.

Benzodiazepines: A class of drugs including Valium widely used for anxiety and sleep disorders, as well as in anesthetic regimes during surgery because of their amnesic effects for the pain and discomfort.

Ascending Reticular Activating System (RAS): Near the base of the brain, a filter deep in the mammalian brain that selectively controls information. RAS controls what you become aware of and what you ignore.

Blood Brain Barrier (BBB): A group of mechanisms that work together to keep some substances, particularly harmful ones, in the bloodstream and to prevent them from passing out of the blood vessels and entering cells in the brain.

Brain: The collection of neurons and supporting tissue within the skull that is responsible for all cognitive processes, including memory.

Brain stem: Sometimes called the reptilian brain, the first part of the brain formed. It determines our level of alertness and handles bodily functions.

Brain lobes: The cortices of the two brain hemispheres are each divided into four areas referred to as lobes. The lobes are specialized in the type of information they store and process. The largest, the frontal lobes, are associated with the performance of higher level cognitive functions, including organization, planning, decision making and problem solving. The parietal lobes extend from the ear to the top of the head. They receive information from touch and are involved in the formation of some memories. The occipital lobes are located at the back of the head. They are sometimes referred to as the visual cortex, and are responsible for visually mediated memory. The temporal lobes fit under the temporal bone above the ears and are involved with hearing, perception and, of particular importance, semantic memory.

Cardiovascular health: When considering the relationship between cardiovascular health and cognitive abilities, most people think of the rehabilitating effects of a stroke. These events can produce profound impairment of memory and other cognitive and motor abilities. We seem to be moving away from the view that cardiovascular factors play only a secondary role in the majority of cases of dementia. It's increasingly apparent that cardiovascular health is also of significance in Alzheimer's disease.

Cerebellum: The part of the brain that controls movement and stores memory related to movement.

Cerebrolysin (CL): The parent drug of N-PEP-12, CL is sold in thirty-five countries for the treatment of a variety of brain insults and diseases, including Alzheimer's disease. A severe limitation on CL use is that it must be delivered through intravenous infusion. CL has been studied by leading teams of neuroscience researchers around the world and shown to have diverse effects that are associated with both acute improvement in learning and memory and in neuroprotection.

Cholingeric: The cholingeric system includes the neurons that release acetylcholine and the neurons and proteins that are stimulated or activated by acetylcholine. Cholinesterase breaks down acetyl-choline into choline and acetic acid.

Cognitive functions: All aspects of perceiving, thinking, learning, remembering, organizing information, planning and conceptualizing.

Cognitive Behavior Therapy (CBT): Developed by Dr. Aaron T. Beck, used to treat depression, anxiety and a side range of psychological disorders. Stresses the importance of thoughts one has and the importance of those thoughts in subsequent feelings and behaviors.

Computerized Axial Tomography brain scan (CAT): Used to detect blood clots, brain tumors, shrinkage of the brain, thinning of the neocortex, and symptoms of Alzheimer's disease, a CAT scan is basically a computer-enhanced x-ray that creates a three-dimensional picture of the body or part of it.

Cortex: The one-eighth inch thick, intricately folded layer of nerve cells that covers the brain's cerebrum. The cortex allows us to remember, to analyze and compare incoming information with stored information, to organize experiences, to learn a language, make decisions and perform myriad other cognitive tasks.

Cortisol: The hormone formed in the adrenal cortex that controls your body's reactions to stress.

Declarative memory: memories for facts or past experiences in life.

Dementia: A deterioration of cognitive functions or intellectual abilities, causing confusion, disorientation, and memory loss for recent events, and interfering with a person's normal daily activities and social relationships.

Dendrites: the branching extensions of a neuron that receive impulses from other neurons and conduct them toward the cell body.

Depression: The emotional state of being sad, often accompanied by difficulty in thinking and concentration.

Dietary supplements: Products developed from naturally occurring substances that can be sold without prescription and used to treat various ailments, including memory loss. Also referred to as "nutraceutical" products. They may not be sold in the United States for the treatment of a "disease."

Drug combinations: Combining drug regimens might cause unusual or different side effects than intended by the individual prescriptions.

Diphenhydramine: Found in many common household remedies like cough syrups or antihistamines, these sedating drugs can be potentially problematic for learning and memory. Benadryl® is the most common brand name.

Episodic Memory: Memories tied to specific events, time and places

Galantamine: One of the five drugs approved in the United States to treat Alzheimer's disease, galantamine is a derivative of the snow drop plant that may have been used more than 3,000 years ago by the ancient Greeks.

Gingko biloba: Sold as a dietary supplement to improve memory, extract from gingko biloba is derived from an eponymous tree that is probably the oldest surviving species on earth, perhaps 200 million years old. Use of leaves and bark from the tree to treat the brain dysfunction is described in a Chinese medical texts dating to 2800 B.C., nearly 5,000 years ago.

Glucose: This simple sugar is the chief source of energy for all the body's cells.

Hippocampus: A critical brain region for information entering memory storage and consolidation and is important for storage of spatial and navigational memory.

Hormone: A chemical compound formed by certain glands and organs. Absorbed into the blood, it influences the function of other parts of the body.

Huperzine A (HPA): An ancient Chinese herbal medicine that is prepared from the Chinese club moss and used to treat many disorders.

HPA is an alkaloid that limits the breakdown of the neurotransmitter acetylcholine and, therefore, raises available acetylcholine levels in the brain. This neurotransmitter is critical for memory and decreased levels are characteristic of Alzheimer's disease and Age-Associated Memory Impairment.

Hypothalamus: The part of the brain that regulates many aspects of metabolism, including hunger, body temperature and reproductive function.

Hypothyroidism: Approximately ten percent of women over sixty-five have clinical hypothyroidism and among substantially older women the prevalence may reach twenty percent or more. The thyroid is a butterfly-shaped gland in the front of the neck, on either side of the Adam's Apple. It is also under the control of the hypothalamus, in the base of the brain. In this case, the hypothalamus sends thyrotropin releasing hormone (TRH) to the adjacent anterior pituitary gland, which then sends thyroid stimulating hormone (TSH) to the thyroid gland which produces the thyroid hormones thyroxine (T4) and triodothyronine (T3). These hormones then travel to specific receptors in every cell in the body, including the brain, and control the rate of metabolism and all the physical and chemical processes that allow growth and maintain body function. Any problem along this route, or damage to the thyroid gland itself, can produce inadequate levels of thyroid hormones, referred to as hypothyroidism. There is substantial evidence that thyroid hormones influence memory. Decreased levels of T4 correspond with decreased cognitive performance and decreased levels TSH are associated with decreased episodic memory performance in healthy older adults. Even thyroid hormone levels in the low range of what is considered normal can produce memory problems. When hypothyroid function is properly treated, it can be very gratifying for patients, their family members and clinicians to see the dramatic improvement in memory and other symptoms that can occur.

Left brain: Reasoning functions such as language are often lateralized to the left hemisphere of the brain.

Limbic stem: The hippocampus, amygdala, and related structures that are involved in motivation, emotion and the transformation of short-term memories into long-term memories.

Long term memory: You might think of long term memory as "everything you know." This could include geography classes from high school, your best friend's face or where she lives, how to fill out a spreadsheet at work, or any of the other information found in the vast memory bank in your head. There are at least two different types of long-term memory: Declarative Memory, or memory for facts or past experiences in life, and Procedural Memory, which is memory for skills. The vast majority of what we think of as information in long-term memory is in Declarative Memory and here we generally divide information into episodic memory or semantic memory. Episodic memory relates to personal experience while semantic memory combines memories to understand concepts.

Lecithin: A mixture of phospholipids that constitute major components of all living cells. (Note: Lecithin does not occur in the body. The phospholipids do.)

Metabolism: The process of turning food into energy.

Mild Cognitive Impairment (MCI): The diagnostic category used to describe people who are not demented, but who score below the expected range for their age on neuropsychological memory tests and who show evidence on clinical interview that memory loss is affecting their ability to function at home or in the workplace. MCI is associated with an increased risk of developing Alzheimer's disease or another dementing disorder.

Mild Traumatic Brain Injury (MTBI): A diagnostic label for memory and attention problems resulting from falls, auto accidents, and blows to the head.

N-PEP-12: A derivative of Cerebrolysin that can be administered orally and that has been shown to improve learning and memory in AAMI. N-PEP-12 has many effects on the brain, including increased glucose availability and utilization and facilitating neuronal plasticity. N-PEP-12 is a dietary supplement because it is derived from natural sources and it is sold in the Untied States under the name MemoProve®.

Neuronal plasticity: A phenomenon in which neurons react to changed conditions by making new connections or using existing connections in different ways.

Neuropeptide: A short chain of amino acids (long chains of proteins) that can function as neurotransmitters or hormones in the brain

Neurophysiology: A part of physiology concerned with the study of functioning of the nervous system. It is closely connected with neurobiology, psychology, neurology, and other brain sciences.

Nutraceutical products: Products that can be sold as "dietary supplements" with little FDA oversight. Some are intended to nourish the brain and protect it from damage as we age and face stresses and insults that contribute to brain aging.

Neurotransmitters: Chemicals in the brain that facilitate the passage of electrical signals from one neuron to another,

Omega-3 free fatty acids (FFAs): A nutraceutical product important for the developing brains of fetuses and children and also the brains, as well as hearts, of mature adults.

Phosphatidylserine (PS): A critical part of the cell membrane in every cell of every living organism. As cells in the brain (and elsewhere else in the body) age, they can become rigid as cholesterol replaces the normal phospholipids. PS administration is thought to improve brain cell fluidity and improve transmission across the cell wall. PS also increases the availability of acetylcholine and affects other neurotransmitter systems that may be implicated in AAMI.

Originally from a bovine source, it was not until the mid-1990s that PS products developed from vegetable sources came to the U.S. market and, whereas PS had been studied as a drug, the DSHEA legislation allowed it to be sold as a dietary supplement for memory loss. PS can be a valuable supplement in AAMI.

Procedural memory: Memory for skills, riding a bike, for example.

Prosthetic Memory Environment: Professor B.F. Skinner often discussed the concept of a prosthetic environment for the brain, just as prosthetic environments are created for those with physical disabilities. He was fond of the notion that, as one ages, one should "rely on memo's not memories."

Remote memory: The repository for "unforgettable" experiences. These may be many decades old, going back to early childhood. Even if some of this memory may not be in our immediate memory, it can often be quickly retrieved with a slight reminder.

Right brain: Music and visual abilities such as spatial manipulation, facial perception, and artistic ability seem to be largely lateralized to the brain's right hemisphere.

Semantic memory: Context free memory that represents general knowledge about the world.

Selective recall: Blocking or failing to recall information that contradicts one's (often negative) beliefs.

Short term memory: The retention of small amounts of information, perhaps five to six bits of information, for a period of seconds.

Sleep apnea: Just one of the many conditions that can contribute to memory loss. A common problem for overweight individuals, sleep apnea is marked by cessation of breathing during the night. It's characterized by loud snoring and gasping and can greatly reduce oxygen delivery to the brain. Each period of breathing cessation lasts ten seconds or more and dozens or even hundreds of these episodes can occur during the course of one night, thus producing symptoms of both memory loss and fatigue the following day.

Synapses: Specialized junctions through which cells of the nervous system signal to one another and to non-neuronal cells. They are crucial to the biological events that underlie perception and thought. They also provide the means through which the nervous system connects to and controls the other systems of the body.

Vinpocetine: A dietary supplement in the United States and a drug in almost fifty other countries. It was synthesized from the blue periwinkle plant in about 1960 and is used to treat a variety of conditions including cerebral vascular ischemia. It may have value in stroke and other vascular disorders that can impair memory and other cognitive functions, but there is no sound evidence that it is effective in AAMI or related disorders.

Working memory: An intermediary memory system where we can hold information just long enough to complete a task, without transferring it into long-term memory. We must keep information in working memory in our consciousness and continue rehearsing it, for example, when remembering a phone number just long enough to dial it.

Appendix 1

Tests of Everyday Memory Abilities
Author: Dr. Thomas Crook

You can take either or both of the simple memory tests in this Appendix and then compare your scores to those of other people your age, or to scores of young adults performing optimally.

Test 1: The First–Last Names Association Test

In this test you will see six pairs of first and last names. Read each out loud and then turn the page and try to write the first name that corresponds to each last name. If you do not want to write in the book, get six or seven blank sheets of paper at this point, and use them to record your answers. You will be given three chances to recall the names. So, let's begin by reading the names below.

First try:

Ellen Wilson

Kathy Stein

Paul Brooks

Elizabeth Morrow

Jonathan Everett

Rick Patterson

Now, turn the page and try to write the first name that corresponds to each last name.

_____ Morrow

_____ Stein

_____ Patterson

_____ Wilson

_____ Everett

_____ Brooks

Now go to the next page and read the same names again.

Second Try:

Jonathan Everett

Rick Patterson

Kathy Stein

Paul Brooks

Ellen Wilson

Elizabeth Morrow

Again, turn the page and try to write the first name corresponding to each last name.

_____ Brooks

_____ Patterson

_____ Everett

_____ Morrow

_____ Wilson

_____ Stein

Go to the next page. Please read the same name pairs out loud again.

Third and Last Try:

Paul Brooks

Elizabeth Morrow

Rick Patterson

Jonathan Everett

Kathy Stein

Ellen Wilson

For the final time, turn the page and write the first name that corresponds to each last name.

_____ Stein

_____ Patterson

_____ Wilson

_____ Brooks

_____ Morrow

_____ Everett

Now please go back and add your correct scores from all three attempts. Then look below and compare your score with those of thousands of other people to whom we have administered the test.

Not so easy, eh? This is a difficult test because, as we discussed in Chapter 1, humans rely very heavily on vision for memory. Unless you could use visualization techniques, as described in Chapter 4, this would have been a purely verbal task and, thus, quite difficult. So, let's see how you did.

Below is the average score for each age group. Please note the clear drop that occurs during the forties and the gradual decline after that.

AGE GROUP	AVERAGE SCORE
18–39	11
40–49	8
50–59	7
60–69	6
70+	5

By the way, women do slightly better on this test than do men.

We will now move on to a test that does have a visual component. In this case we will test your ability to remember the name of someone to whom you are "introduced." This is the most common memory problem in every culture we have studied. So please turn the page and see how well you do.

Test 2: The Face–Name Association Test

Please study the faces and names on the following pages. Say each name out loud as you examine each face and try to temember the name that goes with each face. You have one minute to study the faces.

First Try

Marilyn Rhonda Denise

Derek Julia Louise

Eric Robert Curtis

Identify As Many As You Can

Now please fill in the name of every person you can remember beneath the corresponding photograph. *When you have finished, please go to the next page without calculating your score.*

Second Try

Look at the names and faces again. Study them for one minute, saying out loud the name of each individual as you look at the face. Then turn the page and fill in as many names as possible.

Robert   Denise   Derek

Julia   Curtis   Marilyn

Louise   Eric   Rhonda

Once Again, Identify As Many As You Can

Please fill in as many names as possible.

Go back and check the names against the faces and tabulate the number of correct answers. You can measure your performance against others using the scale below.

Check Your Performance

Please calculate the number of correct answers on each of your two attempts and see how well you performed by looking at the scale that follows:

First Try

If your age is between:	The normal range of correct responses is:
18 and 39	4–8
40 and 49	3–7
50 and 59	3–6
60 and 69	2–5
70 and 89	1–4

Second Try

If your age is between:	The normal range of correct responses is:
18 and 39	6–9
40 and 49	5–9
50 and 59	4–9
60 and 69	3–7
70 and 89	2–6

Appendix 2

Authors: Drs. Marshal Folstein, Susan Folstein and Paul McHugh

(Not intended for self-administration)

The Mini Mental Status Examination (MMSE)

	Score	Points
Orientation		
1. What is the Year?		1
Season?		1
Date?		1
Day?		1
Month?		1
2. Where are we? State?		1
County?		1
Town or city?		1
Hospital?		1
Floor?		1
Registration		
3. Name three objects, taking one second to say each. Then ask the individual to name all three after you have said them. Give one point for each correct answer. Repeat the answers until the patient learns all three.		3
Attention and Calculation		
4. Have the individual spell the word "WORLD" backwards. One point for each correct letter.		5

	Score	Points
Recall		
5. Ask for names of three objects learned in Question 3. Give one point for each correct answer.		3
Language		
6. Point to a pencil and a watch. Have the individual name them as you point.		2
7. Have the individual repeat, "No ifs, ands or buts."		1
8. Have the individual follow a three-stage command: "Take the paper in your right hand. Fold the paper in half. Put the paper on the floor."		3
9. Have the individual read and obey the following: "CLOSE YOUR EYES." (Write it in large letters.)		1
10. Have the individual write a sentence of his or her choice. (The sentence should contain a subject and an object and should make sense. Ignore spelling errors when scoring.)		1

	Score	Points
11. Enlarge the design printed below to 1-5 cm. per side and have the individual copy it. (Give one point if all sides and angles are preserved and if the intersecting sides form a quadrangle.)		1
TOTAL =		30

Scoring

Add numbers. A score of 24 or lower may suggest a consultation with a physician. Do not let a score over 24 override your judgement, however. If the individual in question is having memory problems that are having a clear impact on his ability to function from day-to-day, consultation with a physician should be given serious consideratiion.

Appendix 3

Authors: Dr. Jerome Yesavage and colleagues

(intended for self-administration)

The Affective Ratings Scale (ARS)

Choose the best answer for how you have felt over the past week:

1. Are you basically satisfied with your life?   Yes   No
2. Have you dropped many of your activities and interests?   Yes   No
3. Do you feel that your life is empty?   Yes   No
4. Do you often get bored?   Yes   No
5. Are you hopeful about the future?   Yes   No
6. Are you bothered by thoughts you can't get out of your head?   Yes   No
7. Are you in good spirits most of the time?   Yes   No
8. Are you afraid that something bad is going to happen to you?   Yes   No
9. Do you feel happy most of the time?   Yes   No
10. Do you often feel helpless?   Yes   No
11. Do you often get restless and fidgety?   Yes   No
12. Do you prefer to stay at home, rather than going out and doing new things?   Yes   No
13. Do you frequently worry about the future?   Yes   No
14. Do you feel you have more problems with memory than most?   Yes   No
15. Do you think it is wonderful to be alive now?   Yes   No
16. Do you often feel downhearted and blue?   Yes   No
17. Do you feel pretty worthless the way you are now?   Yes   No
18. Do you worry a lot about the past?   Yes   No
19. Do you find life exciting?   Yes   No

20. Is it hard for you to get started on new projects?   Yes No

21. Do you feel full of energy?   Yes No

22. Do you feel that your situation is hopeless?   Yes No

23. Do you think that most people are better off
than you are?   Yes No

24. Do you frequently get upset over little things?   Yes No

25. Do you frequently feel like crying?   Yes No

26. Do you have trouble concentrating?   Yes No

27. Do you enjoy getting up in the morning?   Yes No

28. Do you prefer to avoid social gatherings?   Yes No

29. Is it easy for you to make decisions ?   Yes No

30. Is your mind as clear as it used to be?   Yes No

Scoring

Assign one (1) point to the answer "NO" for items 1, 5, 7, 9, 15, 19, 21, 27, 29, and 30.

Assign one (1) point to the answer "YES" for all other items.

A score of 12 or more can be associated with depression. You may wish to discuss this possibility with your physician.

Appendix 4

Stress Management

Author: Dr. Thomas Crook

According to the American Psychological Association, you are probably experiencing significant stress in your life if you:

- Are always rushing and often late
- Take on too much and have "too many irons in the fire"
- Feel over-aroused, short-tempered, anxious and/or tense most of the time
- Describe yourself as having "a lot of nervous energy"
- Have "worry wart" tendencies (focus on negative possibilities and anticipate crisis or disaster in most situations)

Such stress can arise from many circumstances in the workplace or at home and can lead to a very long list of physical, psychological and behavioral problems that include memory loss, but also:

- Hypertension and cardiac disease
- Depression and anxiety
- A broad range of gastrointestinal problems
- Migraine
- Neck and back pain
- Immune suppression (more colds, flu etc.)
- Skin problems
- Hair loss
- Sleep disturbances
- Drug and alcohol abuse

The list could go on and on but, suffice it to say that it is important to learn to control the stress in your life.

Let's look first at the acute symptoms of stress. These too are very broad and will vary from person to person or from time to time in the same person. They include:

- Rapid heart beat
- Dry mouth
- Urge to cry, run, or hide
- Inability to concentrate
- "Butterflies" in the stomach
- Feelings of dizziness, anxiety, or doom
- Insomnia
- Sweating without physical exertion (particularly sweaty palms)
- Trembling and nervous tics (usually in facial muscles)
- Speech difficulties

This list too could be extended substantially, but all of us know at least some of these symptoms and can recall them arising from early childhood when we got a poor report card or "got into trouble" with our parents.

A little stress from time to time is probably harmless and can even be quite helpful in motivating us to complete unpleasant tasks but chronic stress must be controlled, lest it lead to memory problems and a long list of other problems, of which some are listed above. So, let us consider some techniques that can be helpful in dealing with stress in your life.

1. *Remove the stressors in your life.* I realize this could lead to bad news for a lot of husbands out there and I also realize that there are not a lot of orphanages around these days so a working mother with a couple of kids will only be able to do so much in this category. However, if you simply write down on a piece of paper all of those people or things that are causing stress in your life, and how much of the total stress in your life is attributable to each (what percent), you will very likely identify at least some important stressors that can be removed. You can often find a more stress-free job, a doctor who does not keep you waiting three hours, a kid who can speed up your computer, or a creative (and legal) extra source of money. Most important, look for peo-

ple in your life who are "toxic" and quarantine or remove them as if they were a computer virus. This sounds harsh, particularly because these people may be family members, but do not accept the long duration of a relationship as an excuse for keeping people who cause you stress in your life. These are the people who cause your stomach to drop a little when you must meet them or take their call, so do what you can to eliminate them from your life. Do the same with the "things" in life that cause you stress.

2. *Simplify your life.* Many of the things and activities in your life that cause you stress are really not necessary. Throw out things and roles in your life that are not productive. If you are not enjoying or profiting (financially, psychologically or spiritually) from an activity, stop doing it. It is very helpful, in this regard, for you to learn to say "NO" when asked to do something that you do not expect to be fun and productive. I remember reading of a gentleman who felt obligated to sit on every charitable board that asked him, including a local chapter of the American Heart Association. As a result he was always running from task to task, place to place, until he died of a heart attack.

3. *Learn to block and replace thoughts causing you stress.* Like all other feelings, the feeling of being stressed is preceded by certain thoughts. They might be something like "I will never meet this deadline" followed by "I will let the boss down" and by "I could lose my job over this" and by "I might not be able to find another job" and "How will I tell my wife" and "I won't be able to support my kids" and so on. You must learn to recognize and break such chains of thoughts. Think about old movies from the 40s and 50s where a woman would become "hysterical" (it didn't happen to men in those days) and someone, usually a man, would slap her in the face, whereupon, she would regain control of herself and rational thought would return. Such therapeutic

slapping is probably not a great idea today, if it ever was, but it does illustrate that when negative thoughts begin to form chains based on catastrophic thinking, you may need to shock yourself back to reality. A simple rubber band around the wrist is a useful device for this purpose. Simply and masochistically draw the rubber band back and release it, allowing it to sting the inside of your wrist. This shock will generally stop the cascading thoughts as your brain shifts to focus on the pain. Then take several deep breaths, sit down and, assuming the stress is not coming from an oncoming train or a moray eel about to strike your throat, examine the thoughts you were having just prior to the onset of your feelings of being stressed. Write each thought down and then try to answer each thought rationally and put it in perspective. In the example above, you would ask "What is the probability that I will miss the deadline?" "Will I disappoint my boss and, if so, how important is that?" Tell yourself, "I can find another job, and one that wouldn't cause me so much stress. Maybe this stress is a good thing and a sign that I should start looking." Generally the stressful feelings will greatly diminish before you even reach the "How will I feed my dog?" level of irrationality.

4. *Replay a peaceful memory.* Go back in your life and try to remember the four or five times when you felt the greatest happiness and peace. Rehearse each of these memories in great detail, including detailed visualization of the scene, who was saying what to whom, or what you were thinking if you were alone. Include sounds around you and smells. Now, as we discussed before, when the stressful feelings arise, sit down, take a couple deep breaths, close your eyes and insert the mental DVD of one of those scenes. Enter the memory just as if you are experiencing it again. Use a second DVD if necessary. Many of you will find this a very effective means of dealing with stress.

5. **Relax through progressive muscle relaxation.** Practice this technique every day and see if helps relieve tension and stress. First, lie in bed or sit in a comfortable chair. Pick a time and place where you will not be interrupted for at least 20 minutes. Now, proceed as follows:
   - Clench your fists tight, then slowly relax them
   - Bend your hands inward, then slowly relax them
   - Tighten your biceps as hard as possible, now slowly relax
   - Bring your shoulders upward toward your ears, hold them there, then slowly lower
   - Tighten your chest muscles by pulling your shoulders back, then bring shoulders slowly forward and relax chest muscles
   - Tighten your stomach muscles as much as possible, feel the strain, then slowly relax the muscles
   - Tighten your buttocks, hold, then slowly relax
   - Pull back the toes on your left leg as far as possible, then slowly relax the toes
   - Stretch the left leg with the toes pulled upward, then slowly relax
   - Stretch the left leg with the toes pushed downward, then relax slowly
   - Do the same three exercises with the right leg and toes
   - Arch and then slowly relax your back
   - Bend your head forward as far as you can and then slowly relax
   - Bend your head as far as possible to the right, then relax slowly
   - Repeat to the left
   - Clench your jaw, the relax
   - Frown disapprovingly, then slowly relax

6. **Do what ever relaxes you and consider it an investment in your health and well-being.** Go fishing, practice yoga, bake cookies, play ball with the kids, have a cocktail—whatever helps you relax will not only be good for your memory but will keep you around a few more years so that your kids and grandkids will remember you.

Appendix 5

Healthy Sleep Tips

From: The National Sleep Foundation

1. *Maintain a regular bed and wake time schedule including weekends.*

   Our sleep-wake cycle is regulated by a "circadian clock" in our brain and the body's need to balance both sleep time and wake time. A regular waking time in the morning strengthens the circadian function and can help with sleep onset at night. That is also why it is important to keep a regular bedtime and wake-time, even on the weekends when there is the temptation to sleep-in.

2. *Establish a regular, relaxing bedtime routine such as soaking in a hot bath or hot tub and then reading a book or listening to soothing music.*

   A relaxing, routine activity right before bedtime conducted away from bright lights helps separate your sleep time from activities that can cause excitement, stress, or anxiety that can make it more difficult to fall asleep, get sound and deep sleep, or remain asleep. Avoid arousing activities before bedtime like working, paying bills, engaging in competitive games, or family problem-solving. Some studies suggest that soaking in hot water (such as a hot tub or bath) before retiring to bed can ease the transition into deeper sleep, but it should be done early enough that you are no longer sweating or over-heated. If you are unable to avoid tension and stress, it may be helpful to learn relaxation therapy from a trained professional. Finally, avoid exposure to a bright light before bedtime because it signals the neurons that help control the sleep-wake cycle that it is time to awaken, not to sleep.

3. *Create a sleep-conducive environment that is dark, quiet, comfortable and cool.*

   Design your sleep environment to establish the conditions you need for sleep—cool, quiet, dark, comfortable and free of interruptions. Also make your bedroom reflective of the value you place on sleep. Check your room for noise or other distractions, including a bed partner's sleep disruptions such as snoring, light, and a dry or hot environment. Consider using blackout curtains, eye shades, ear plugs, "white noise," humidifiers, fans and other devices.

4. *Sleep on a comfortable mattress and pillows.*

   Make sure your mattress is comfortable and supportive. The one you have been using for years may have exceeded its life expectancy—about 9 or 10 years for most good quality mattresses. Have comfortable pillows and make the room attractive and inviting for sleep but also free of allergens that might affect you and objects that might cause you to slip or fall if you have to get up during the night.

5. *Use your bedroom only for sleep and sex.*

   It is best to take work materials, computers and televisions out of the sleeping environment. Use your bed only for sleep and sex to strengthen the association between bed and sleep. If you associate a particular activity or item with anxiety about sleeping, omit it from your bedtime routine. For example, if looking at a bedroom clock makes you anxious about how much time you have before you must get up, move the clock out of sight. Do not engage in activities that cause you anxiety and prevent you from sleeping.

6. *Finish eating at least 2–3 hours before your regular bedtime.*

   Eating or drinking too much may make you less comfortable when settling down for bed. It is best to avoid a heavy meal too close to bedtime. Also, spicy foods may cause heartburn, which leads to difficulty falling asleep and discomfort during the night.

Try to restrict fluids close to bedtime to prevent nighttime awakenings to go to the bathroom, although some people find milk or herbal, non-caffeinated teas to be soothing and a helpful part of a bedtime routine.

7. *Exercise regularly. It is best to complete your workout at least a few hours before bedtime.*
   In general, exercising regularly makes it easier to fall asleep and contributes to sounder sleep. However, exercising sporadically or right before going to bed will make falling asleep more difficult. In addition to making us more alert, our body temperature rises during exercise, and takes as much as 6 hours to begin to drop. A cooler body temperature is associated with sleep onset. Finish your exercise at least three hours before bedtime. Late afternoon exercise is the perfect way to help you fall asleep at night.

8. *Avoid caffeine (e.g., coffee, tea, soft drinks, chocolate) close to bedtime. It can keep you awake.*
   Caffeine is a stimulant, which means it can produce an alerting effect. Caffeine products, such as coffee, tea, colas and chocolate, remain in the body on average from 3 to 5 hours, but they can affect some people up to 12 hours later. Even if you do not think caffeine affects you, it may be disrupting and changing the quality of your sleep. Avoiding caffeine within 6-8 hours of going to bed can help improve sleep quality.

9. *Avoid nicotine (e.g., cigarettes, tobacco products). Used close to bedtime, it can lead to poor sleep.*
   Nicotine is also a stimulant. Smoking before bed makes it more difficult to fall asleep. When smokers go to sleep, they experience withdrawal symptoms from nicotine, which can also cause sleep problems. Nicotine can cause difficulty falling asleep, problems waking in the morning, and may also cause nightmares. Difficulty sleeping is just one more reason to quit smoking. And never smoke in bed or when sleepy!

10. *Avoid alcohol close to bedtime.*

Although many people think of alcohol as a sedative, it actually disrupts sleep, causing nighttime awakenings. Consuming alcohol leads to a night of less restful sleep.

If you have sleep problems ...

Use a sleep diary and talk to your doctor. Note what type of sleep problem is affecting your sleep or if you are sleepy when you wish to be awake and alert. Try these tips and record your sleep and sleep-related activities in a sleep diary. If problems continue, discuss the sleep diary with your doctor. There may be an underlying cause and you will want to be properly diagnosed. Your doctor will help treat the problem or may refer you to a sleep specialist.

Appendix 6

The Most Common American Last Names (and Cues to Remember Them By)

From: Psychologix, Inc.

Abbott	& Costello; a "butt" (cigarette butt)
Adams	Adam's apple
Allen	allen wrench
Anderson	Hans Christian Anderson character; Anderson window
Andrews	Andrew's Air Force Base; hand drew
Bailey	bay leaves; Bailey's Irish Cream
Baker	baker's hat—rolling dough
Baldwin	bald (head) "1"; Baldwin organ
Barry	berry
Bell	bell
Bennett	bayonet
Bernstein	burn stain (scar); conductor's wand
Black	black color
Blake	lake, blink
Brooks	brook
Brown	brown color; Charlie Brown
Burke	burr
Burton	button; tons of burrs
Butler	butler
Campbell	Campbell's Soup
Carson	Johnny Carson; Carson City; car & sun
Carter	Jimmy; Carter's children's wear; cart her
Clark	Clark candy bar

Cohen	cone
Collins	collie; Tom Collins drink
Cooper	chicken coop
Cunningham	sly ("cunning") ham; Richie Cunningham
Daniels	Jack Daniels; lion's den; coonskin cap (Daniel Boone)
Davis	Bette Davis eyes
Donald	Donald Duck
Douglas	Douglas fir tree
Edwards	Edwards Air Force Base; King Edward (crown)
Ellis	Ellis Island
Evans	Bob Evans
Feinberg	fine (ticket); iceberg; bird
Feldman	felt on a man
Fisher	fisherman; fishing pole
Flanagan	Father Flanagan; "flan-again"
Foster	foster home; Foster's Lager
Gardner	gardener
Gilbert	gills on Bert (from "Sesame Street")
Ginsberg	gin on iceberg
Goodwin	good wind
Graham	Graham Cracker; Grandma
Green	green color
Hall	hallway; Hall's Cough Drops
Hamilton	ham weighs a ton
Harper	harp player; Harper's Bazaar
Harris	hairless
Harrison	hairy son; hairy sun
Hartman	heart man; heart-shaped moon
Henderson	hen under son
Henry	hen on rye; hen with ray of sun
Hopkins	Johns Hopkins; kin hopping
Jackson	jacks with sun as the ball
Jacobs	Jacob's Ladder

James	King James (crown); Jesse James
Jenkins	junk in
Johnson	John's son; Howard Johnson's; Johnson & Johnson
Jones	jeans
Jordan	Jordan River; country; Jordan
Kaufman	cough man; man coughing
Keller	Helen Keller; killer; killer whale
Kennedy	JFK; RFK; can of dye; Kennedy Airport
King	crown; king piece from chess
Klein	climb; Calvin Klein
Kramer	creamer
Lang	long; laying
Larson	arson; larceny
Laurence	Laurence of Arabia; Laurence Welk
Lee	leaf; lei
Levine	leaves on a vine
Levinson	leaving son; leaving sun
Levy	Levi's Jeans
Lewis	St. Louis Arch;
McDonald	McDonald's golden arches; duck (Donald)
Martin	martini
Maxwell	Maxwell House Coffee
Meyer	admire; mayor; mare; my ear
Michaels	my calls; mike (microphone) kills
Miller	miller; Miller Beer
Mitchell	shell in a mitt
Monroe	man rowing; Marilyn Monroe
Moore	mooring; more of
Morris	Morris the Cat; more ice
Murphy	Murphy's Oil Soap; more fees
Nelson	wrestling hold
North	compass; North Pole
Oliver	olive
O'Neal	O kneel

Owens	owing; O wins
Palmer	palm tree; palm of hand
Patrick	hat trick; rich pats of butter
Paterson	pat her son
Paul	pall bearer; pull
Perkins	coffee percolating; Perkin's restaurants
Perry	pairs; pair of E's
Peters	P tears
Philips	full lips; Phillip's screwdriver; milk of magnesia; fill 'er up
Quinn	wind; queen
Randall	handle
Raymond	ray of sun on mount, mound
Reynolds	Reynold's Wrap
Richards	rich herds
Roberts	robbers
Robinson	robin's son
Rogers	Mr. Rogers; Rogers & Hammerstein
Rosen	rose in vase
Rosenberg	rose in (ice) berg
Ross	Betsey Ross (flag)
Rubin	reuben sandwich
Russell	Jane Russell (full figures); rustling leaves; cattle rustling
Ryan	rye (in mouth)
Samuels	some mules
Schmidt	mitt (as in catcher's mitt)
Schneider	sniper; snide; cider
Schultz	Charles Schulz ("Peanuts")
Schwartz	warts; shorts
Scott	scotch, Scott towels, Scot
Sears	Sears Roebuck
Sherman	sure man, shoreman; Sherman tank; the March
Simpson	Bart (cartoon character)

Sloan	loan; slow on
Smith	blacksmith
Spencer	suspenders
Stern	stern (a boat)
Steward	steward; hard stew
Sullivan	Ed Sullivan; sullied van
Swanson	swan son; swan song; Swanson's TV dinner
Tate	tight; Sharon Tate
Taylor	tailor
Thomas	tom-tom (on ass); mass of toes
Thompson	Tom's son
Turner	Tina Turner; spatula (turner)
Tyler	tiler; tile her
Victor	winner; "V" (victory sign)
Wagner	wagon
Walker	baby walker; old person's walker
Wallace	wall of ice
Walters	wall of tears; Barbara Walters
Warner	warn her; Senator Warner
Watson	watt's son, what son?; Dr. Watson
Webster	web stir; dictionary
Weiss	wise; ice
White	white color
Williams	will yams
Wilson	Wilson tennis balls; basketballs
Winston	Winston Churchill, Winston cigarettes
Wright	write; right
Young	baby; young person

Index